WHO'S WHO of CATS

JOH

D1414136

WORKMAN PUBLISHING, NE   RK

WHO'S WHO of CATS

Library of Congress
Cataloging-in-Publication Data

Who's who of cats / edited by John R. F. Breen.

p.   cm.

ISBN 1-56305-629-1 (paper)

1. Cats–United States—Biography.
I. Breen. John R. F.

SF445.5.W515   1944   94–1330

636.8'00973—dc20   CIP

Workman Publishing Company, Inc.
708 Broadway
New York, NY 10003
First printing May 1994
Manufactured in the United States
10 9 8 7 6 5 4 3 2 1

INTRODUCTION

As we all know, cats now rule the world, which is why a Who's Who of cats is so timely. A hundred years ago cats were lowly mousecatchers, just beginning to infiltrate our homes; now, however, ask them to catch a mouse and they just look at you, like what century are you living in? It's not exactly clear when the cats took over. Historians generally place the event around 1870, although there are reports of cats in the Australian outback taking orders from humans as late as 1892.

Today cats are the equivalent of sultans. We, the human servants, bring them exquisitely prepared food, stroke them on demand, and generally attend to their every need. We are mere beasts of burden, staggering under successive loads of kitty litter. Like other large, lumbering creatures, we will eventually go extinct and then the cats will have to train those dim-witted dogs.

While reading this book, you may occasionally wonder, "Huh, how did that cat get in *Who's Who of Cats*? What's it done?" This is exactly the point. The cat has usually done nothing, which is a big thing in the cat world. Cats pride themselves on their ability to do nothing. In this way *Who's Who of Cats* is different from a human *Who's Who,* which usually sets forth criteria based on merit, importance, and great deeds. To a cat these things are so ... mundane. Anyone can put on a good face in public and make a couple of large donations, thereby becoming an important figure. These things are far, *far* beneath a cat's dignity.

In the cat world, the real issue is control. Concepts like altruism don't exist—they have been relegated to lesser species, such as dogs. In fact, *accomplishments* themselves are not highly regarded, since they usually involve some kind of effort. Consequently, the selections in this book are based on the cats' own criteria and reflect the new world order in which dogs are altruistic, loyal, and helpful to humans; humans are altruistic, loyal, and helpful to cats; and cats are altruistic, loyal, and helpful to nobody.

Originally appearing in *Who's Who of Animals,* these biographies were written by human friends or indentured servants who patiently followed their felines around for years and, like modern-day Boswells, steadfastly recorded their every deed. Collected here you will find the biographies of many of the most distinguished and prominent cats in the world. You will undoubtedly find that they fill you with a deep sense of awe.

ABDUL
SAN DIEGO, CALIFORNIA

Abdul was born under the raised floor of a command-and-control facility in Saudi Arabia. Some workmen took him and his littermates from under the floor, cleaned their eyes, and then put them right back where they'd found them! I was working there at the time, and I wasn't too surprised when this terrified kitten turned up on my desk a few days later. He's still with me and not totally tame. Now seven years old, he's a shorthair with orange-and-white fur

ACE BAIRD
LEWISVILLE, NORTH CAROLINA

With the build of a linebacker and the sensitivity of a child, Ace tempers arrogant independence with a fondness for cuddling. This fourteen-pound gray domestic shorthair was originally a blood donor at a veterinary hospital, where he gave new life to countless others. Now his childlike enthusiasm gives life to everything he comes in contact with, from a crumpled piece of paper on the floor to the hearts of everyone who meets him; that is, everyone but the mailman, whom Ace has been known to growl at, like a dog, on more than one occasion.

AJ BOWDEN
TAMPA, FLORIDA

At five years of age and fifteen pounds, AJ's favorite activities include eating, and eating, and eating! Of course, several naps are taken between his many meals. Unlike most cats, AJ is an attention hog and likes to be around people all the time. Unfortunately, due to his eating habits, he is a bit too big to fit in a lap comfortably—but he never stops trying. AJ's favorite toy is his companion cat, Sydney. He spends hours every day washing her face. It never seems to be clean enough to suit him.

ALEXANDRA O'NEILL
IRVINE, CALIFORNIA

Alexandra O'Neill—
 She never misses a meal.
 She eats baby food from a china plate.
(She thinks the turkey and lamb are great.)
You ask how do I know?
Because she tells me so.
Alex can speak to me in her own special way.
"I'm hungry" and "Good morning" are some
 of the things she can say.
She's a tiger-striped cat.
Four years old, and a little fat.
She loves to run, jump and leap.
But most of all, she loves to sleep.
In Alex I'll have a lifelong friend.
I'll treasure her until the very end.

ALLIE
JACKSONVILLE, FLORIDA

Allie is a three-year-old black cat who likes to pretend she's a dog. She sits and shakes hands on command. She can even be coaxed to sit up and beg, but only if food is involved. (At least she has her priorities straight.) Her favorite activities are eating and sleeping. Her least favorite activity is being chased by her friends Diggy and Randa, who are dogs. They like to lick the back of her neck until it's coated in dog saliva, which acts like styling mousse and makes her hair stand up like a mohawk.

ANGEL COOKIE
NORFOLK, NEBRASKA

Angel Cookie is an unconditional friend, companion, and pal. Each year she visits the first graders I teach for our Pet Unit. She sits on the piano when we sing Christmas carols and is there on the steps to greet me when I get home. Angel had a rough start in life. She and her brother were born on our family farm in a cold rain and snow storm; they were saved by my parents, and Angel came to live with me! People may let me down, but not Angel. She is always there for me. Angel Cookie is a true friend.

ANNIE MARIE DUBOIS
REDWOOD CITY, CALIFORNIA

Annie was abandoned when she was three days old. Found by her adoptive mum, Pam DuBois, Annie was bottle-fed every three hours until she could eat on her own. She would go everywhere with Pam, and people would often look surprised when they found a kitten wrapped in the receiving blanket instead of a baby. This was done to keep Annie alive. Because of her tough beginnings, Annie and Pam have formed a very special bond. Annie, also called Princess, is the apple of Mom's eye. A true rags-to-riches story.

ANNIE THOMPSON
FRESNO, CALIFORNIA

Annie is a thirteen-year-old Persian cat who ran into our carport out of a rainstorm in 1980. She travels with us in the motor home and thinks she is the "Official Greeter" in the parks we visit. In 1983 we entered her in the Pet Therapy program conducted by the Education Department of the Central California SPCA. Annie has been working ten years now, visiting hospitals, nursing homes, and schools on a regular schedule. The happiness she brings just by being there to be petted and offer unconditional love makes us very proud of her.

ANONYMOUS LARSEN
IRON STATION, NORTH CAROLINA

Anonymous is our miracle tabby cat. For three years he was diagnosed with Feline Leukemia. This year he became one of only thirty percent of cats that have cured themselves of this disease. At twelve and a half pounds, he is very healthy. He loves to roam outdoors, chasing butterflies and catching mice. He also loves to be inside, curled up on the couch or stretched out in front of the fire. Anonymous has a habit of hiding around corners and then clawing our ankles or pouncing on the dogs. A game of chase usually begins and we all get a good laugh.

AOK INDIGO SUNRISE
DAYTON, OHIO

Sunni is a Blue Point Himalayan who does a great "Mad Dog" impression. Anyone who wanders too close to one of the windows is greeted by Sunni's bulging eyes and a mouthful of gleaming white teeth chattering together. He loves to jump out at people who are inside the house as long as they do a good job of acting surprised. If you don't act surprised, don't pick him up and ask for a kiss because he'll stick a paw over your mouth (the universal sign for no kisses).

ARTHUR HOWARD
ALEXANDRIA, VIRGINIA

A rthur is a white Flame Point Himalayan with pudgy paws, gorgeous blue eyes, and a loud, commanding voice. He is a purr-box, purring constantly from the moment he lifts his head from the pillow next to his owner, Donald, to the time he retires for the night after a strenuous day of basking in the sun and munching on Tender Vittles. Arthur loves to be brushed, but even with all the grooming, balls of his fur cascade across the floor like tumbleweeds. Arthur has the profile and regal bearing of a lion as he strides proudly through his Virginia garden.

ASHES
MARTINSBURG, WEST VIRGINIA

Ashes is a living example of why people hate cats. Of course, she hates people, too—so it's even! The problem is, even her vet hates to see her come into the office. Ashes is a seven-year-old half-Siamese. She was named for the color of her coat and because we thought she would turn out to be a beautiful cat (like Ashes in the Cinderella story). As the story goes, Ashes is only beautiful to me. She loves to hide in closets and scare people who are not expecting to see her (usually my husband).

ATHENA (GODDESS OF WAR) COURTNEY
VERNON, CONNECTICUT

A thena is a three-month-old female tortoiseshell kitten who enjoys attacking Spazz and Spotty, the two cats whose realm she moved into. She also enjoys causing headaches for her humans. She loves to steal pens and knock over everything in her path. She also loves sneaking laps of coffee from her humans' cups in the morning. Athena's favorite toy is a giant stuffed horse; she likes taking off his saddle, sunglasses, and muzzle, and carrying them around the house. The humans whom she has part ownership of are James Courtney and Joely Dorval (whose pillow she enjoys sleeping on at night).

AUBREY CAT ROBB
CHICAGO, ILLINOIS

Named after the well-known portrait artist Aubrey Davidson-Houston, Aubrey Cat is an elegant gentleman—a tiger-striped Maine Coon. Playing with his tail is his most strenuous activity, followed by napping in front of the fire. He has choreographed a marvelous "Dinner Dance" which he performs before receiving canned food. His favorite sport is bird-watching, and he communicates with each species with a different sound.

BABY COMMANDO KITTY TODD
ESCONDIDO, CALIFORNIA

Baby is a black Siamese with two personalities. She is loving at night, when she sleeps under the covers, and a terror during the day. Her favorite toy is a small piece of candy shaped like a banana. She sits at the window and "chirps" with the birds. She'd rather eat on the counter instead of the floor, and she prefers water running from the tap. Baby's best asset is her ability to jump—she tries to look out the peephole in the door, making people think there's always someone at home!

BARNEY REBEL
WATERFORD, CONNECTICUT

We brought Barney home from my sister's farm after Sam died. My husband and I are elderly, and Sam, our black Burmese, had grown old with us. Barney is an independent orange tabby who allows you to pet him only if he wishes. He does not like our grandchildren or me but will sit with Mr. Phillips. Always looking for trouble, he has changed our whole life-style. We have a sign on our front door that says: "Please Be Careful. Our Cat is Possessed by the Devil and Does Not Go Out!"

BAUDELAIRE (A.K.A. GODDESS, PAPRIKA, DIVA)
NEW YORK CITY, NEW YORK

Baudelaire is believed to be the incarnation of Madonna's mother. She is also a tarot reader and a psychic. Her favorite band is Soul Asylum. She drinks coffee, and her favorite ice cream is Ben & Jerry's Chocolate Chip Cookie Dough. Baudy is the most beautiful cat. She's a Seal Point Siamese with ruby eyes and a fierce voice, and a glamorous attitude like nobody's business. This year she plans to star in her own calendar.

BEARCAT BARTON MISNER
WEBBERVILLE, MICHIGAN

BearCat is six years old, weighs fourteen pounds, and has gray-and-white fur and big yellow eyes. His diet consists of tuna every morning, gourmet cat food every night, and Dairy Cat on the weekends. At dinner his tastes are too wide to mention. He visits the garage and sometimes gets beef jerky. His teeth and body get brushed three times a week. He always goes on vacation with us, of course, with the air conditioning blowing on him. He sleeps with me every night, and occasionally I get my hair washed. We love him more than words can say.

BEETHOVEN LEARNARD
GRANITEVILLE, SOUTH CAROLINA

B eethoven is a typical Siamese cat, except that he was born deaf. As a result of his deafness, he was put up for adoption by his owners. Originally very aggressive, he has become a very lovable cat. When four orphan kittens were introduced to the house, he took to them immediately, caring for them as if he were their mother. He still washes them daily and "calls" for them if he cannot see them.

BEEZUS LOUISE ("FOUR SOCKS") DUCLAYAN

BROOKLYN, NEW YORK

Beezus is a small, sturdy (cow-like, in fact) kitty, predominantly black with some white. She was found at a mechanic's garage in Brooklyn and was first called "Grease Monkey" because of her oil-splotched fur and engine smell. She was quite ill at the time, but she soon recovered. Now two and a half years old, Beezus loves to play with her Cat Dancer toy and to open and close doors. She just says "no" to catnip. She is named after a Beverly Cleary character and always comes when her name is squealed at a pitch painful to the human ear.

BELLE LITTLEJOHN (A.K.A. MAMA FATSO)
DENVER, COLORADO

Belle, our striped tabby, is twelve years old. Given to us as a kitten, she was born outside and a little wild. She preferred the outdoors up until about a year ago, then decided the house was a pretty neat place after all. She still goes outside but only to roll in the dirt, catch some sun, and let the other neighborhood cats know she's still one tough kitty even though she's overweight and has three teeth. She and our dog, Ginger, naturally tolerate each other after eleven years together.

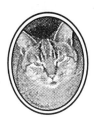

BENJI
DURHAM, NORTH CAROLINA

Benji is twelve years old and Mr. Curiosity. He wants to know who is visiting and lets them know this is his house. He is very protective and should a serviceman be around he'll growl and hiss very loudly as if his attack is imminent. We know it's all show, but they don't. Benji lives with Monty, our black Lab, indoors but really only tolerates him. We sometimes feel he thinks of dogs as a lower form of life! Benji is still active, especially when birds are around. His favorite pastime now is lap sitting.

BERT AND CHESTER BEAL
AUGUSTA, MAINE

Bert was adopted from the Bangor (Maine) Humane Society as a wee "cowhocked" kitty and lived with Susan. After Susan married David, they moved to Big D, Texas. Bert flew down with Delta after they settled their apartment. Four years later, they moved to Clinton, New York, and finally settled in Maine. Since Bert was a "housecat," they went and adopted another tiger kitty to keep him company; this is Chester. They amuse themselves with *many* toys and watch birds at the feeder. Now that Andrew Mitchell Beal (a human baby) has arrived, I'm sure life around the house will be even more exciting!

BIGFOOT RAY
CRETE, ILLINOIS

Bigfoot is a gold-colored longhair. He is very affectionate and likes to sleep in our bed with his paws touching our arms. He meets us at the back door when he hears the key in the latch. Gene will whistle and Bigfoot will come running, no matter where he is in the house. He has a long, pink-and-white-striped sock that he carries around between his paws and meows real loud. He follows us around the house and likes to be in the same room with us while taking part in his favorite pastime: catnapping.

BILL WIDDERS
SANTA ROSA, CALIFORNIA

Bill is a beautiful, remarkable cat who was found in a garbage can eight years ago. Funnier by the day, he insists on doing everything the opposite of our other five cats. He walks with the dog, drinks from a glass, and talks constantly. He truly *can* communicate and thinks he's human. Bill Widders has survived endless accidents, illnesses, and surgeries. His spirit is like a kitten's. He entertains our family every day with his antics and new tricks. Bill is a special member of our family and has given us great love and devotion that we all cherish.

BLACK KITTY ("FAT BLACK") YOERGER
LAS VEGAS, NEVADA

Black Kitty, our slightly overweight stumper Manx, has beautiful long jet-black fur, a small white chest, and four white feet. She first came to us while trying to hide from a crazy bird that would dive-bomb her and attack her back. She would not fight back, only cower at our door. Soon she came to depend on us as we would bring her in on cold nights and feed her daily. So when we had to move, she came with us. I know we haven't regretted bringing her, and I think she's just as happy being with us.

BOBO TYRONE SHAW
SANTA FE, NEW MEXICO

Bobo, age twelve, is a black-and-white tabby kitty who weighs twenty-one pounds. Bobo was firstborn of the litter, and he has never shirked the responsibilities associated with this. His hobbies include eating, sleeping, and rolling on his back to show off his large white tummy. He loves exploring forbidden places and taking a walk with the family. Bobo particularly enjoys meeting new people and makes friends easily. He co-starred in the film *New Mexico—Our Place* with his younger brother, Doobie, and shared the Best Actor award with him.

27

BONKERS JUSTICE
NORTH ROYALTON, OHIO

onkers is a beautiful gray cat. He is nine years old and just loves to sit in your lap. Of course, the best time to sit in laps is when you're trying to read the paper. Whenever I open the refrigerator, he has to stick his head in and see what's there. He never gets anything, but likes to check it out anyway. He lives with six Siberian huskies and three other cats. He loves to rub up against the huskies when they're sleeping. They just look at me as if to say, "Gee, Mom, get him out of my face."

BONNIE MEWMAN BRACKETT
MANHATTAN, NEW YORK

A Scottish Fold by breeding, Bonnie is a native of Detroit, Michigan. She is white with several prominent black spots on her back and a black mask around her yellow-green eyes. Her owner is Barbara, to whom she is utterly devoted. A human in fur, Bonnie is a highly vocal advocate of greater independence for cats with short ears. Passionately devoted to travel, she annually vacations at her home in South Carolina and frequently weekends in Vermont. An instinctive naturalist, she has a keen interest in entomology. Her numerous interests include bird-watching and practical sleep research.

BOO-BOO CLARIDA
VENTNOR, NEW JERSEY

B oo-Boo is four years old. He is smoky gray with green eyes. Boo-Boo loves to be petted and brushed, and he gets very emotional if you don't pay constant attention to him. He loves the outdoors, and at night he has a favorite green blanket he likes to sleep on. His favorite food is squid.

BOOTIE
PORTLAND, OREGON

We adopted Bootie from the Humane Society. She's about five years old and is a tortoiseshell color. She always acts grouchy and only lets you pet her when she wants it. We think it's just an act. Her favorite spot is on top of her scratching post, looking out the window. We're very glad that we adopted her instead of a kitten. We love her very much.

BOOTS HUGHES
EL SEGUNDO, CALIFORNIA

Boots, a six-year-old domestic shorthair, is gray in color and has white boots on her feet. Her other names are Ankle Biter (she likes to play by biting your ankles) and Hair Licker (she also likes to lick your hair while you try to sleep). She is a very affectionate cat and loves to sleep on her back with all fours straight up in the air. Her favorite friend is Mousey, a stuffed mouse. Actually, Mousey doesn't have any stuffing left. She's "loved" him too much. We love Boots, too!

BOOTSIE
BUELLTON, CALIFORNIA

Bootsie is a nondescript gray mottled cat—the kind of cat that no one notices. But what she lacks in appearance, she more than makes up for in manners and good breeding. She is feminine and polite, quiet and regal, never pushy or demanding—content to sit on a chair and observe the world go by. A shorthaired version of a resident cat, she appeared one day at our house, walked through the door, hopped into a window seat and decided she was home. She was so unobtrusive that no one noticed until one day somebody in the house counted kitty noses and asked, "Where did this one come from?"

BRAT-CAT ("FRAIDY") KUBELDIS
HUNTINGTON BEACH, CALIFORNIA

B rat's the middle cat, the third out of five born in the spring of 1981. She's afraid of anything that moves or makes a noise. She loves to climb, scratch on her scratch pole, and jump to places the other cats wouldn't think of going! She also loves to rip apart catnip bags in her spare time. Brat-Cat is the neurotic of the group. She loves TLC but is afraid to come to you for it. When you pick her up, she squeaks at first but then quickly melts on to your lap. She is the best snuggler.

BRIEZZY BRIELLA BROWN
ROSELLE PARK, NEW JERSEY

An excellent pet, Briezzy lives with one German Shepherd/Husky, four Teacup Chihuahuas, a parrot, an assortment of finches and canaries, ten parakeets, a bunny, and three guinea pigs. She is happy and never harms any of the other animals. She loves belly-rubs and treats. She never scratches or plays too rough. I do think she is slightly confused as to her identity—she lives with so many other animals and never sees another cat. She is good company. Briezzy loves to "talk" and tells me everything. We love each other much.

BROWNIE LYNCH
CAMBRIDGE, MASSACHUSETTS

Brownie is mostly black with some white on her neck, stomach, and paws. Sometimes we call her a tuxedo cat. (She just needs to find a bow tie.) Her true name is either Hieronymus or Bosch—we're not sure which one. She's half Siamese; however, the only obvious indication of this heritage is her meow, which is very expressive. She rules her household and faithfully guards her cat territory, allowing no other cats across her boundaries. We generally find ourselves following her orders, but we don't mind because we know she loves us dearly. Purr, purr, purr.

BUD JONES
PLAINFIELD, INDIANA

Bud is a four-year-old orange Persian with the most precious disposition. Everything he does is always gentle and slow, and he'll let you pet him when he's in the mood. He looks like he ran into a wall, his face is so flat, but everyone loves him. In the summer he gets a new "do"—the "lion cut"—which is funny to look at but cool for Bud. He gets a bath on a regular basis, and when he gets blown dry he'll raise his arms for you. He is a very special cat and is loved very much.

BUDDY
SALT LAKE CITY, UTAH

Buddy, a parking lot stray, is just less than a year old. His big copper eyes and orange coat make him quite the handsome young man. Usually mellow, he can be quite obnoxious and insistent on talking back. His days are spent lounging at the top of his condo, but he also enjoys sunbathing nude and playing seek-and-attack with his brothers. Other favorite pastimes include stealing the ball, wrestling the plants out of the windowsill, and taming the arm that pets him. Always purring in confidence, he knows that his mom and dad are there for the comfort and convenience of their feline children.

BUDDY (A.K.A. BUDDY BUDENSKI) SAMPLES
CLINTON TOWNSHIP, MICHIGAN

B elieved to be the runt of the litter and cast out, Buddy is a shorthair from New Jersey. On the first night we took him in, he curled up at my side and purred nonstop the rest of the night through. His proudest accomplishment was learning how to take a running start, soar through the air, and cling to the curtains very near to the ceiling and play Super Cat. He loves chasing and fetching his rabbit's foot for us to throw out again—I guess he's playing the great hunter. He also likes to chew on toes!

BUFFINGTON C. SHERLOCK
HOUSTON, TEXAS

Buffington C. (for Cat) was born on Pearl Harbor Day several years ago. He has a white mink-like fur coat, which he proudly wears everywhere—even in Texas summers. Like his mother, Advance Cat, Buffington has eyes of different colors. A sporting type, he catches tossed items in midair or bats them back. He retrieves, boxes while standing erect, and sleeps on his back. He endorses important papers with a row of tooth marks along the margin. Oreos are his favorite dessert. Buffy enjoys wearing ribbons, and his likeness appears in an oil portrait with his owner, a Houston philanthropist.

BUMPERS (A.K.A. BOOBIE UBIE, BUMPER DUMPER, RUNT SUMPER)
MILLINGTON, NEW JERSEY

B umps is a small cat, with white, orange, and black stripes. She is easily spooked but has a friendly, kooky personality. She got her name from her habit of greeting by bumping heads. Wild and mischievous in her younger days, she has mellowed although she persists in sneaking into rooms that are off limits. She used to like jumping into the washer until someone started it not knowing she was inside. When chilly, she snuggles up to a warm body as close as possible. She misses her best friend, Wilhelmina, who died in 1987.

BUNDLEBRANCH COLLETT
PORT WASHINGTON, NEW YORK

B undlebranch (Bunny or Rabbit, for short) is a Seal Point Siamese. She is eight years old and eight pounds heavy, with big blue eyes and chocolate-colored fur. Bundle only likes you if you have a chocolate-coated vanilla ice cream readily available for licking. Her next favorite food is banana. Bundle thinks she's human—a princess, no less—so she decided when she was a kitten to use the human toilet instead of a litter box. To this day, she's never missed. Being a princess, however, she never flushes; that part is left to the next person who enters the bathroom.

BUSTER AUGUSTUS SCHMIDT
BALTIMORE, MARYLAND

B uster's origins are quite mysterious. Magically, he appeared in the garden of a Federal Hill row house. All the neighborhood felines reverently deferred to him for his benevolent leadership. Upon retirement, *he* decided to move inside and make the little home his castle. Buster's preferences and sophisticated tastes are quite pronounced, as is his stylishly symmetrical tiger-striped physique. Opera, Italian cuisine, and real estate investments are his passions. He is a member of numerous professional societies and frequent-flyer programs. He continues to graciously share his estate with his ward Zoro while entertaining and educating his two adopted humans.

BUSTER MADDONA
GILBERTSVILLE, PENNSYLVANIA

Buster, age five, is a gray tiger cat with white paws and neck. He is overly friendly and nibbles when being ignored. He also loves cat treats, which he catches in midair and then throws around. One of Buster's favorite games is to climb onto the bed and then jump into a basket near the bed so that it slides across the floor. He also likes to drink iced tea out of glasses.

BUSTER PETTLER
HOLLYWOOD, CALIFORNIA

A bedraggled gray-and-white stray kitten followed Pamela and Robert Pettler to their home in the Hollywood Hills one wet winter night in 1989. He ran into their house and refused to budge. Today he is a fat (seventeen-pound), much-cosseted member of the Pettler household. Pamela is a writer and producer in TV, and Buster's photograph has appeared in sitcoms with such noted personalities as Jane Seymour, Jamie Lee Curtis and Lesley-Anne Down. Buster has now become a famous Hollywood cat.

BUTCH THE MACHO CAT
BALLWIN, MISSOURI

N o one knows his birthplace, nor why his tail is only an inch long, but Butch the Macho Cat guards his territory fiercely, challenging feline trespassers to single combat. He has never been defeated. Neutered several years ago, Butch is so macho he hasn't noticed yet. He is also a feline financier, counting his wealth in people. He owns or holds substantial shares in nine humans. Butch's reputation is formidable; he even gets fan mail from the St. Louis Zoo's great cats. That's macho! That's Butch!

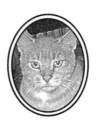

BUTTON JORAT
PALO ALTO, CALIFORNIA

Button was rescued from under the hood of a car. She is a tortoiseshell who looked like a football when she was little. She's still little, even though she's a year and a half old now. Her mom thinks she's the cutest cat that ever was, but her Auntie Chris thinks she looks like Bluto. Her favorite sport is chasing tinfoil balls and hiding them; when last checked, she had a stash of about fifty, plus a few other assorted treasures. Button is always waiting by the front door with a nose rub ready for her mom.

BYNKII ROTSTEN
SYLMAR, CALIFORNIA

Bynkii is a ten-year-old male Abyssinian, ruddy with gold eyes. Everyone who sees him wants to take him home. It must be his friendly attitude and "puma" look. Maybe you've seen Bynkii in newspapers or magazines: he's the trademark for his owner Michael's animal-rights law practice in Encino, California. Bynkii is also a comedian. He puffs up like a monkey and runs sideways, knocks things off the wall to wake you up, and opens cupboards by standing up on his hind legs, taking hold of the door, then walking backwards until it opens.

CALICO RANEY
COCOA, FLORIDA

Calico is a unique cat. She has six toes on every paw and uses her front paws like little hands. She is very intelligent and friendly and loves to play fetch. She also loves to hunt and talk, and she knows just how to manipulate me in order to get anything she wants such as a bowl of milk or tuna fish. She's like a child to me and tests me to see if I'll scold her for doing things she's not supposed to do. Everyone loves her, and even the neighbors sneak her in their house on occasion to give her little treats.

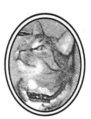

CALLIE (RAT CAT) CORK-SAMPLES
CLINTON TOWNSHIP, MICHIGAN

The living, breathing terror of Clinton Township, this small calico cat packs so much energy that it's a shame there is no way to harness it. She loves attention and to get underfoot, and follows us everywhere we go when we're at home. For all her terror, she's a loving cat who enjoys your lap for a nap and burrows under your chin at night to sleep. She has also decided that the refrigerator is her very own private domain.

CALLY (CALLYANDRA) POTT
ST. LOUIS, MISSOURI

C ats, like all animals, can be such clowns, such distracters, playing peek-a-boo with you on your dining room chairs as you eat or "walking the tightrope" on the rim of the tub as you bathe. My Cally is not only a silly one, but also a great teacher. She does not teach philosophically; rather, Callyandra Pott guides by being a good model. Early to rise, she eats . . . then calls for her tub faucet water to wash her face, lies in the sun for vitamin intake, and finally off around the house for some exercise. She has me doing the same.

51

CAPPUCINO HENNICK
OCALA, FLORIDA

Cappy is an AKC three-year-old blue-cream Seal Point Persian whose ambition is to live the good life. He enjoys Saturday cartoons, steak, playing fetch, and sleeping on his suitcase. His loving nature shows daily with purrs and cuddling. The highlight of his day is the time he spends with Keri and Dan, screaming and yelling for food. (Unfortunately, they can't resist, which has resulted in a *slight* weight problem.) Never was there a more talkative feline—he speaks his mind whether you want to hear it or not. He's an irreplaceable part of our lives, but don't tell him that!

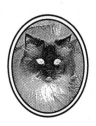

CARAPOO ST. BUTLER ROBB
CHICAGO, ILLINOIS

A lso known as "the Princess" because she's clever at getting her way, Carapoo is an elegant lady with long black fur and a fluffy tail. She likes to be covered up with her afghan and insists on ice water. Since her oral surgery, she sometimes is called "One Fang Kitty," although she does not prefer that name. She of course is extremely beautiful—she gets about twenty-two hours a day of beauty sleep.

CASSIOPEIA ("CASSIE") MONTOYA
LITTLETON, COLORADO

C assiopeia is a three-year-old calico kitty with beautiful orange and black markings and a white face and paws. She was rescued from the Lakewood Animal Shelter when she was one year old, and since then has grown from a shy cat who hid in the cupboards, especially with people around, to an affectionate, playful pet who literally throws herself on you if she likes you. She enjoys opening drawers on the under dresser but spends most of her time lounging on the waterbed.

CAT THOMAS
MURRYSVILLE, PENNSYLVANIA

C at belongs to my brother, and yes, he named her. She is about two years old. She is black and white and looks like an Oreo cookie! Cat is a purebred Manx. She answers to "Kitty." She pretty much lays around, eats, and sleeps, but gets in these moods where she just rockets around like a maniac. And when she gets near the dog, she hisses and spits, which isn't pretty. When she purrs, she sounds like a 350 engine! Take my word, you'll never eat meat or drink milk in this house without the cat getting some of it!

CECIL ("CE CE") GRAFF
BROOKLYN, NEW YORK

Born May 27, 1992, this adorable red tabby Maine Coon won the hearts of his owners from the start. He's affectionate and loves to play, especially at 4:30 A.M. on the weekends. His favorite toys are his stuffed mice and pinky (a little ball with a bell), both of which he likes to throw around and bring into the bed. Cecil enjoys traveling and supervising the driving. He also helps with the laundry; he makes sure his socks are cleaned by placing them with the rest of the clothes on laundry day.

CELIA
CAMBRIDGE, MASSACHUSETTS

Celia, a three-year-old longhair with tortoise-shell coloring, is an indoor cat. Very sweet-natured, loving, and playful, she enjoys running after, fetching, and returning crumpled-up balls of paper to whomever she's suckered into the game. When feeling frisky, she grabs onto my legs and we do a bit of sparring—with Celia up on her two back legs batting at my hands with her front paws. Most people find Celia quite beautiful, although a neighbor once compared her to a barn owl because of her round eyes and wedge-shaped head. She's a terrific cat!

CHALIS McCONNELL
OCEANSIDE, CALIFORNIA

Born April 1985, Chalis is an orange-and-white tabby who loves attention and lots of affection. She's very sweet, and when my husband or I lie down on the couch to watch TV, she goes to sleep on our chest. She starts purring as soon as you touch her. I love cats—in this hectic world, they are very calming. Chalis also likes to hold a conversation and chase the light from the flashlight.

CHAN
SHOREHAM, NEW YORK

Chan was an Applehead Seal Point Siamese who loved to perform tricks. He could turn doorknobs with his paws, would slide down a very steep banister, and walked proudly on his leash down the street. He was a devoted mate to Ming Toy and fathered many litters of kittens. Ming allowed Chan to assist her at the birth of their kittens by bathing them. He would take over their care to allow Ming time for herself. When I went to camp one summer, Chan mourned for me so severely that he had to visit me at camp to prove I was all right!

CHANDON STEWART
VALLEJO, CALIFORNIA

C handon loves to sleep in the baby's room under the crib, and even though she has no kittens of her own she is very distressed when baby Kelly cries. Her only exercise is chasing flies in the house and being chased by her twin brother, Moet. (The twins got their names from a bottle of French champagne.) Chandon is a fourteen-pound American Shorthair, three and a half years old. She likes to play soccer with almost anything that you happen to drop on the floor.

CHANGI'S BEASTIE OF KIDEZE
MINNEAPOLIS, MINNESOTA

Changi's Beastie is a Singapura cat, just over one year old. His name fits him around the house and show ring. He loves to wrestle with the other cats in the house, especially if they're asleep. He runs to the refrigerator every time anyone moves, but he must watch his "girlish" figure. He never stays in one spot very long and enjoys watching baseball on TV—he tries to catch the batter on the screen. He is holding his own in the Cat Fancy show scene.

CHAPMAN ("POOH") BURNS
BIRMINGHAM, ALABAMA

Pooh is a three-year-old registered Himalayan Persian who has an extreme aggressive aversion to people other than myself. What makes him unique, however, is his nightly ritual of drying my hair! Every evening after showering, I sit on the couch to watch the nightly news. Pooh immediately jumps up and starts to lick my hair until it's dry. I can barely hear the TV over his loud purring. (This is the *only* time he purrs.) My one attempt to break him of the ritual resulted in bites to the head, rather than licks, so I elected to accept it as a sign of affection.

CHARLIE YODA
LA GRANDE, OREGON

Charlie is a gray striped tabby who was born a "dumpster cat." Although she lives inside now, she often cases out the door waiting for opportune moments to escape. She'll suddenly flop over in midstride as if she's been shot by a passerby, then lie in the "dead Badger pose" that makes her all the more unique. Chuck will eat anything but bananas and toothpaste, so she's always on her "cat diet" to try to slim down. In the morning, she taps you on the forehead and steps in your eye until you get up and feed her.

CHARLOTTE ANN HOLDEN
SHERMAN OAKS, CALIFORNIA

Charlotte Ann Holden is a most extraordinary cat. She is a supremely feminine creature, a butterfly tabby with green-blue kaleidoscope eyes. An amazing huntress, she honors us with a gift each day. She enjoys a good meal and always finds the last beam of sun in which to stretch her fur-lined body. Charlotte is loyal and kind, with a pixie in her soul. She is a gift we all cherish.

CHEYENNE THIEL
ANN ARBOR, MICHIGAN

Cheyenne is the cutest little kitten. She is multicolored with four white socks and the most adorable mask of color on her face. Her new mother brought her home on, appropriately enough, Mother's Day. She has made herself at home with her mom (Carolyn) and her new friend Chelsea. Cheyenne will chase her shadow for hours, not quite understanding why she can't seem to catch it. Playing with the tassels on a rug or with Chelsea's tail will fascinate her endlessly. She is definitely a welcome addition to the family.

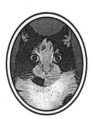

CHIAUN MATEO BOO-BOO KITTY
THORNTON, COLORADO

hiaun came into the world April 4, 1992, and is glad he did. A five-pound British Shorthair with copper eyes, he begins his day by snuggling between Eric and Marlene and purring extra loudly to wake them up. Once this is accomplished, he enjoys lying in bed without moving a muscle while the bed is made over him. Next it's off to the bathroom to spy on his humans while they take a shower; when they're done, he jumps into the tub and pounces on the whirlpool created by the draining water. Another fun-filled day has begun.

CHILE (PEPPER) WHITEHEAD
CASPER, WYOMING

Pepper is an eleven-pound old-style farm cat, but a Siamese. He's a good mouser and friend to Spice (a Cocker). His talents extend to opening doors, playing with toys, and watching TV. He rings a bell to go outside. He likes to follow Spice on dog walks and enjoys greeting you on the sidewalk at the end of a workday. His farm training wakes us up at 5:00 A.M. or earlier. He guards the waterbed, sort of, and likes to be petted just before he eats. An all-round good chap for a friend.

CHITTERS
TOLEDO, OHIO

Chitters was my beloved cat for fourteen years. She was white with gray-brown markings and had the softest head and cutest paws. Her favorite pastimes were cuddling and window watching. Her greatest fear was the organ music from *The Phantom of the Opera*. She liked dogs and birds. She even brought a live baby bird to me at 3:00 A.M. and then showed me where the nest was so I could put it back. There will never be another like her. Rest in peace, Chitters. I miss you.

CHLOE BALLARD
IOWA CITY, IOWA

Each of the five Ballard felines is an American Shorthair of unknown but obviously extraordinary lineage. Chloe, at six, classic black and white with white mittens, is the *grande dame* of the group. Nobody messes with Chloe. Mac and Maggie, five, are gray tabby twins that squabble like human siblings. Willie, three, is marmalade and white, largely overweight, and a darling boy. His best friend is Kiss, the fearless year-old calico baby who was an accident. Her human had gone to the pet store to buy cat food, but she forgot about the food and drove home with tiny Kiss.

CINDERELLA LAW
WHARTON, NEW JERSEY

We rescued Cindy from the animal shelter two years ago and have loved every minute spent with her. She's white and black, and her favorite activities are eating, sleeping, sitting by the window, and watching squirrels. She has the peculiar habit of waking us up at 4:00 A.M. for food even if her dish is full! Although Cindy is quite chubby (fourteen pounds), she does her share of playing and getting into mischief. She loves to crawl into any box half her size. Finally, Cindy's most important quality is her affectionate personality and the love she gives us every day.

CINDY ROO GAGLIANO
PORTLAND, OREGON

Cindy Roo is three years old and has the markings of a chinchilla Persian. She is a very gentle cat, with a frown that lets you know when she's not a happy camper. She is very loving and hops instead of just running—that's how come the Roo. She likes to be held and walked but is not a lap cat. Playing with a rubber ball is her forte, and lying with my other cat. She likes to be left alone, comes when I call her name, and most definitely loves her treats. Cindy loves to carry a small soft object around. She meows very little.

CLARENCE LEE CROCKARELL
GRANITE CITY, ILLINOIS

C larence came into our lives by dint of his tenaciousness and Marge's soft heart. He *was* a puny, yellow-furred creature who begged until he finally got his way. He loves being outside and will visit the neighbors' homes—yet wants to be "free" to roam. Clarence was named for his somewhat cross-eyed appearance (like the lion) and uses his cuteness to win hearts. He stays warm in the winter in his little igloo and loves his summer screen house on the deck. We are all glad he came and stayed. If you're in the area, stop by—Clarence will meet you on the steps. P.S. Bring tuna!

CLARK GABLE MILAM
ROXBORO, NORTH CAROLINA

C lark just showed up one night, skinny, hungry, and obviously abandoned. He came to the right place, as I graciously took him in. When I first saw him, I couldn't decide whether he was the most beautiful cat I had ever seen or the ugliest. Now that he's filled out, I've come to the conclusion he's the most beautiful. He's a long, black-and-white eighteen-pounder. Entertaining he is. Every morning he drags all the towels in the house, and sometimes rubber gloves, into my bedroom. My philosophy is that he must think he's sweeping the floor with the towels.

CLEO
MAUMEE, OHIO

C leo is an adorable and sociable black-and-white cat. At age one, she enjoys chasing and retrieving her ball and furry mouse, going outside with her "dog-brother" (she also nurses from him), riding in the car, stealing rubber bands, playing in the rain, and thoroughly investigating shopping/grocery bags and purses. When not busy with her activities, Cleo spends time visiting our fish, parakeet, and finches under watchful eyes. Then it's on to her favorite naptime spot (a glider rocker in front of the sliding glass door). Cleo is truly a delight and loved a lot.

CLEO OBERMIRE
NORFOLK, NEBRASKA

C leo is an extremely playful and friendly calico who will welcome everyone as a friend—if they give her enough attention! Her favorite person is Gary. She loves to sleep with him and show him how to play Nintendo. She also loves dessert, especially sweet rolls, and sitting in the window and watching the world go by.

CLEOPATRA BREEN
BRANFORD, CONNECTICUT

Cleopatra is a black-and-white cat who acts like a princess yet is also Mommy's little shadow. At age seven, she spends most of her time indoors asleep in the sun, but will venture out and tag along as a helper whenever her mom goes outside. Cleo comes when she is called and has a recognizable vocabulary with which to communicate her thoughts. Her cutest moments are usually in the morning, when all she wants to do is stay in bed and cuddle—hence her nickname, "Cuddle-bunny."

CLEOPATRA PACHECO
HALF MOON BAY, CALIFORNIA

Cleopatra is a gorgeous and, of course, highly intelligent brown-and-black tabby with a white underside and an adorable white spot on her back. She is a petite seven pounds. Her personality, energy, and friendship have transformed her owner into an absolute cat fanatic (ask any of her friends). Cleopatra loves bell toys, Pounce goodies, climbing in the Christmas tree, spending time at the beach, and sleeping in. Her first birthday, March 27, 1992, was spent at a party in her honor with cousins Tricia, Tabby, Mateo, and Callie. The party theme was . . . Minnie Mouse!

CLIFFORD BOWMAN
WEST MILFORD, NEW JERSEY

Cliff is not your average black domestic shorthair. Rescued from the local animal shelter at six weeks of age, he was brought into a household containing two large dogs. Not one to be pushed aside, Cliff became the twelve-pound leader of the pack. He is a warmhearted, lovable cat who charms everyone he meets, except the vet. He will come when called, beg for a treat, or warm a lap when in the mood; otherwise, he is an aggressive watch cat, protective of his family.

CLINGER MERRITT
CLERMONT, FLORIDA

C linger, a large part-Siamese cat who looks like a purebred, earned his name not only from his long claws but also from the family M*A*S*H buff. He has a terrible temper and bad disposition (dogs beware!) but loves the person who takes care of him, even going as far as to let her dress him in doll clothes. A very private cat, he never allows anyone to watch him go to the bathroom.

CLUSETTE S. NUGENT
JAMISON, PENNSYLVANIA

C lusette is a Calico Cat Princess. A very classy street-smart feline, she has ruled two neighborhoods and challenged many. At the ripe age of nineteen, Clusette can still jump on counters in a single bound. Her master talent is training dogs, as she has lived with about ten dogs in her years. A lot of admiration goes to the outside girl who has survived people coming and going in her life, as well as having one litter at the age of six months, when named Cluseau and thought to be a boy. MEOW TO YOU!

CLYDE ("THE BUM") KUBELDIS (A.K.A. OREO)
HUNTINGTON BEACH, CALIFORNIA

Clyde was born in May of 1980. The second of five cats, Clyde is Mr. Class. Mellow, unshakable, he helps bring some order into the household. His favorite toy is a Chinese yo-yo, and he enjoys getting high on catnip. A neighborhood favorite, he makes his rounds each evening, greeting special neighborhood friends as they come home. Clyde hates hairball medicine and has to be forced to take it. He retaliates by unplugging any power cord within reach.

COCO JOHNSON KISLAK
MIAMI, FLORIDA

Coco is a white Angora who has a documented age of twenty-two years—surprisingly enough since she once fell eight stories, was hit by a car, and survived a battle with a large police dog. She is still beautiful, though arthritic, and has traveled as far north as Maine and even outside the country. President Bush personally once inquired as to her health.

COCOA
BUELLTON, CALIFORNIA

Cocoa was the lone survivor of her litter. Her mother's milk dried up, and her owner didn't notice until it was too late for all her siblings. She is a beautiful, lean Siamese cat, dark chocolate brown with ocean-blue eyes. We bought her when she was six weeks old, unaware that her chances for survival were slim. Perhaps due to early trauma, she grew into a paranoid cat, racing through the trees, lounging only on rooftops, trusting no one, peering suspiciously at us as though we were Siamese-eating humans. Cocoa is Cocoa, and we love her just the same.

COCOA MOSKOWITZ
LYNBROOK, NEW YORK

C ocoa is a beautiful black lap cat with big green eyes and triangle ears. She's afraid of everything (including mice) except her family. When she was first adopted, Cocoa was tiny, scrawny, and could barely squeak, but after years of loving care she's now . . . small, moronic, and clumsy! When she jumps onto a windowsill, she frequently trips and falls; when she drinks milk, she gets white drops all over her face; and her idea of hunting is watching squirrels through a window with her teeth chattering. We love Cocoa very much and would never *really* send her out on Halloween (heh-heh!).

CONRAD
WATERFORD, CONNECTICUT

onrad, age eight, is a gray-and-white tiger cat. His favorite pastimes include eating, sleeping, and bird-watching. He shares our home with his daughter, Lady VanHeusen White. Most of the time he is sociable and enjoys a lot of attention. In a contest run by our local newspaper, Conrad was given honorable mention as First Runner-Up for Most Ferocious Cat. His size fools many people, but deep down he is very gentle. He has a special place in our hearts and our home.

COONEY HANSHAW
YARDLEY, PENNSYLVANIA

Four-month-old Cooney is a semi-longhair who looks like a raccoon with white highlights. Being the newest addition to our family, he has taught us all the virtues of patience. Trouble is his middle name. From taking the toilet paper on a house tour to taking laundry out of the basket—he's off. He's a nonstop cuddly wild thing who can't meow but squeaks. His favorite toy is a silk flower he carries around in his mouth—although everything goes in his mouth. He's fascinated with water—if there's water, there's Cooney. Our special joy, Baby Cooney.

COTTEN CAT SULLIVAN
NEWARK, OHIO

C otten is a snow-white longhair with greenish-blue eyes that glow in the dark. One of her favorite things to do is to "wallow" in the mud or "climb" under a car just to make her owner mad. She is a pain to keep clean. She has two other hobbies. One is to roll around in the sun. She does it so much that her owner says, "I tell you, that cat's solar-powered!" The other is to hunt mice, rabbits, and other prey and put them on the front porch steps!

COUGAR WINTERQUIST
RAYTOWN, MISSOURI

Dubbed Mr. Personality by those who love him, and Pain-in-the-you-know-what by those who don't particularly like cats, Cougar has never met a person he didn't adore. Originally an only child, he was raised thinking he was a dog and his favorite pastime used to be long walks on his leash with his human mom. Now that he has a little kitty sister, he has taken an interest in more feline pursuits like upending garbage cans and eating house plants. A twelve-pound bundle of mischief, Cougar is definitely the best cat around!

CRICKETT CAZATT
BELMONT, CALIFORNIA

C rickett is a leggy calico born to cat-mom Sherbie. She's a bit fanatical about a tidy home like her owner, Dorothy, and wouldn't be seen in one of those grocery bags or empty boxes others leave around. When enticed with a bag on the floor, she merely takes a sniff and meows her disapproval at the mess. Crickett loves to talk and is a real bug- and fly-chaser. She loves the hunt but handles being hunted differently. Whenever chased by a human, she'd rather fall on her side than run. She's no fool—she gets petted every time!

CUDDLES MARIE MILLER
AMERICAN FORK, UTAH

C uddles was raised in a rambunctious home and as a kitten was often carried in a Great Dane's mouth! When given to her present owner at age one and a half, she discovered "the good life" and lived up to her name. A black-and-white shorthair with green eyes and unusually silky fur, Cuddles is exceptionally responsive, loving, and intelligent. She likes to be held like a baby, and her owner had to learn to write left-handed to get any work done. Now eight years old, she still acts like a playful kitten much of the time.

CUSTARD LOU BRUNER
CHICKASHA, OKLAHOMA

E leven-year-old Custard is a breed known as the Odd-Eyed White, with one green and one blue eye. Whenever a family member calls my name, she'll go to my room to get me. And when the phone rings she'll knock the receiver off the hook to silence it. She likes to see who's at the door and is always the first one there. She's playful in the morning, but after lunch she goes to sleep in the bedroom. Her favorite toy is the ring from the top of a milk container.

CYRUS SHAH-EN-SHAH BAADE
WASHINGTON, D.C.

C yrus, a white Persian with two gorgeous Paul Newman blue eyes, is the cat who put "finicky" in the book for felines. His sleep requires quiet and comfort, his food is hand-mixed and always *fresh*, and lastly his kitty litter must remain clean. Cyrus vacations in south Florida for the winter and spends the summer months in Rehoboth Beach, Delaware. He enjoys sitting on any reading materials.

DAISY YOUNG
WASHINGTON, D.C.

Found sixteen years ago as a kitten in an alley, abandoned with a broken jaw and starved to skin and bones, Daisy adopted Daddy on sight. She literally climbed up his body into his arms (and heart). Having missed a growth stage, she remains little but compensates with the heart of a lioness. She has survived five operations with no loss of vigor—she even insisted on climbing a fence while still under the effects of anesthesia! She loves attention and play; no day is complete without attacking a roll of paper towels and having a chase. Daisy's indomitable spirit is an inspiration.

DAKOTA JAMES WRENCH
GODWIN, NORTH CAROLINA

Cody (short for Dakota) is the regular, run-of-the-mill generic gray cat. I found him, abandoned, at a local store after school on September 9, 1992. He was about three months old at the time. Cody was either born deformed or was hurt at an early age, because he could hardly walk upright and his right paw was curved inwards. Now, after time and care, he no longer falters when he walks and can run and enjoy nature with the best of them. Ever since he became part of my life, Cody has proven to be my best friend.

DALAI LAMA
ALTON, ONTARIO, CANADA

Dalai Lama is a Himalayan beauty who had a personality bypass. She has no offspring, and none are expected. She has a common stepsister whom she detests. A Buddhist, she follows the religion of her namesake, the Dalai Lama. Her favorite pastime is sleeping on her little electric blanket. She has a pet ball that goes everywhere with her. Dalai uses her litter box when no pillows are available. Although she winters in Palm Beach and summers in Canada, she shows no appreciation for creature comforts provided by the people she owns.

DALTON FOUNTAIN
JONQUIERE, QUEBEC, CANADA

Dalton, Yolanda Fountain's seven-year-old shorthair, wears his stripes with the pride of a gladiator. Kind and patient with small dogs, his favorite pastime is stalking and beating up large dogs—a sport he pursues with a vengeance. After each encounter, he fastidiously cleans each of his huge six-toed paws to remove all traces of his dastardly deed.

DAZZLE BORN
INDIANAPOLIS, INDIANA

Dazzle spent her kittenhood cowering in the shadow of her more rambunctious brother, Razzle. She was adopted when she was a year old, and in her new one-cat home she blossomed into an affectionate, playful, and protective pet. Dazzle is a longhaired calico who enjoys chewing and scratching wicker furniture, eating shedded fur, looking out the window, and Kitty Kisses. Although she likes tuna cat food, her favorite things to eat are vegetable soup and soy sauce.

DEIRDRE MCCONNELL
OCEANSIDE, CALIFORNIA

Deirdre is a little Scottish Fold kitty, born in April of 1990. She has mackerel markings, sort of like a tabby, with a beautiful white chest. She is very shy and has her own little section of the house that she thinks is all hers; she'll yell at the other cats if they come near her area. She is very sweet and has a small gurgling voice. She has her own Garfield bed that she loves to sleep, hide, and play in.

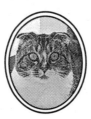

DERF MEERSMAN
SILVIS, ILLINOIS

Derf, a fourteen-year-old yellow-and-white tabby, is partial to his dad but once in a while likes some love from his mom. Every night after they go to bed, he can be found in the living room meowing at full lung capacity and dragging his blanket. He always lets them know when it's time to eat. Ice cream is his favorite.

DESDEMONA BALLMAN
POTOMAC, MARYLAND

D es is a beautiful black six-year-old. Her coat is shiny, and just below her chin is a furry patch of white hair. She is notorious for catching mice and then leaving their remains for someone else to clean up. Des does not take kindly to strangers or even family members—her love goes only to my mother and me. Des spends her summers at the Jersey shore. On cool, sunny days one can find her lounging on the deck, and on very hot days she can be found stretched out on the cool bathroom tile.

DESTINY DICKENS
TAMPA, FLORIDA

Not long ago, Destiny celebrated her seventeenth birthday. Since kittenhood, she has enjoyed a McD. cheeseburger treat on her birthday. She is a tortie-and-white shorthair with a black mask like a raccoon's. She is a lap-sitter and talker, an indoor cat who has lived in luxury and safety. Her parents and littermates died of a virus shortly after she came to live with me. Her name is Destiny because she arrived the same year that a beloved old tortie, named Vallerie, passed away.

DESTROYER SIMPSON
FLUSHING, NEW YORK

D estroyer, the elder of twin cats, is a year-old bicolored tabby with white markings on his feet and nose. He weighs about twenty pounds and loves to eat, which contributes to his large size. One very interesting thing about Destroyer is that he sits up on his butt the way people do. He is the aggressive one of the pair and loves to get into bags.

DIAMOND (IN THE ROUGH) BROWN
BROOMFIELD, COLORADO

D iamond, our brown tabby, rules the house with a velvet paw. She meows to go out and jumps on the screen door so the banging will tell us she wants in. She likes company while she eats and will drink only from a quart canning jar. Tolerant of children's poking fingers and dogs' inquisitive noses, she expects to be treated with respect and we comply. Diamond taught me that every cat is the best cat it can be and that is how it should be with humans, too. Our Diamond is as strong and precious as any gemstone.

DICKENS WATERS
LAKE STATION, INDIANA

Dickens is a shaded silver American Shorthair whose regal appearance and engaging personality endear him to everyone who comes in contact with him. His favorite place to be is in someone's lap, being petted and watching television with his human friends. He also loves to sit on his perch and look out the picture window to see the bird feeder and watch squirrels eating corn. Although he's the largest of our feline friends, Dickens seems to be the most babied by his human servants as well as by his feline and canine friends.

DIMITRI WILLS
TACOMA, WASHINGTON

*D*ashing *I*nquisitive *M*ystifying *I*ntuitive *T*errific *R*egal *I*ngenious. Dimitri's that and more! He's white with one blue eye, one gold eye, and a "puff" (tail) to die for. Rescued from a shelter, he quickly adjusted to "the good life." Eating is his favorite activity. When Mom isn't administering treats, Dimitri just runs to Grandma—with an "abracadabra," she becomes entranced and treats suddenly appear. When outside, Dimitri loves a good game of "Chase That Bird." He came into my life when I needed him. Needless to say, I'm thankful and I sure love him!

DINYA ("THE DEENS") MANN
NEW YORK, NEW YORK

B rooklyn-born Dinya, an orange-and-white thirteen-year-old tabby, is also known as "The Mean Deen" because, although declawed, she terrorizes everyone—other cats, dogs large and small, children and mature adults—with her intense dirty looks. Her vet hastily donned his asbestos gloves to deal with this delicate eight-pound feline "just in case." But to her mom she's the sweetest, most loving, affectionate thing (privately, behind closed doors, of course).

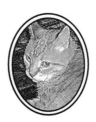

DIVA MARIE BROGAN
DENVER, COLORADO

Diva is a black-and-white cat with a loving personality. She makes herself comfortable on anyone's lap or shoulder. It's not unusual for her to trail a family member around the house like a puppy. Diva is especially attached to her brother, Murphy, and manages to manipulate him into following her every wish. Her favorite activities include clawing furniture (especially couches) and carrying makeup sponges around in her mouth. Diva is five years old. She was a St. Patrick's Day baby and is a very spoiled little girl.

DOOBIE GABLE SHAW
SANTA FE, NEW MEXICO

Doobie, age twelve, is an orange Abyssinian tabby kitty who weighs nineteen pounds. His mother, Pico, was a beautiful calico, and he has two brothers and two sisters. His favorite hobbies are swimming, (accidentally) birding, kneading, and purring. He has a bank account of his own where money he earns from catching mice and gophers is deposited. When necessary, he also enjoys chasing small coyotes and dogs off his property. Doobie recently starred in the film *New Mexico—Our Place* and won an award jointly with his brother Bobo for best actor. He plans to continue his acting career.

DOUGLAS FUR DUCKLES
BERKELEY, CALIFORNIA

A lmost sixteen, Douglas Fur is a sleek gray-and-white cat of great distinction. Fur used to be very quiet, living his own life with decorum and discretion most of the time, but lately he has taken to coming into the house at night, prowling around while making very loud and long pronouncements in the dark, and then going to sleep. Douglas Fur and his dog, Michele, get along famously since neither eats the other's food.

DRAGON
FAYETTEVILLE, NORTH CAROLINA

Dragon, a small black shorthair from Texas, was brought home by our dog, who also helped her fight off her adversary. Dragon is a healer. She is very adept at "laying on of paws": whenever anyone is ill, she'll stay with them until they're feeling better. Dragon had two litters of kittens in her youth. She said eight was enough. Despite her size, she is quite feisty and always has a comment for any given subject. She loves to talk on the phone and can clearly say "Hello." She has converted many an unbeliever!

DUBBIE ("DUB-DUB") BREEN
DEDHAM, MASSACHUSETTS

Dubbie was fondly nicknamed "Gub-Gub" after Dr. Doolittle's pig because he liked to eat so much. Dubbie was rather large. His belly hung down so low it swept the floor when he walked. Once, being a friendly cat, he tried to greet a trick-or-treater at the door on Halloween. The little boy ran away crying about the "dog." His other favorite pastime was to sit on top of the kitchen chair and swat at Timmy (our other cat) and Bessie (our dog) when they walked by. He was a character . . . much loved and fondly remembered.

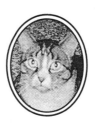

DUCHESS PUDD
RED BANK, NEW JERSEY

"The Pudd," a regal Seal Point Siamese, has reigned in her household for nearly a dozen years. Being something of a recluse, she spends her golden years snoozing in her favorite chair or snuggled in a lap. Duchess Pudd is a connoisseur of chicken and prime rib, and favors her personal blanket and the warm clothes from the dryer. She demonstrates an extensive vocabulary, responding uninhibitedly to human touch or conversation. Above all, this great lady loves to purr along, chin to chin, while being serenaded by a chorus of "You Are My Sunshine."

DUDLEY "STUDLEY" HINCK
CHEYENNE, WYOMING

Dudley, a four-year-old tan Persian, is a very distinguished cat and lets everyone know it! He struts around his house as if he were a king. Dudley likes to sleep on the bed or on his kitty perch so he can see what's going on outside. He loves to chase and play with his sister, Kotte. He can sit up and beg for treats when he wants to be *extra*-specially cute for his mom, Alison.

DUSTER WILSON
LAS VEGAS, NEVADA

Duster is a light ginger-colored cat with white paws and a white front. He was raised on a farm in Washington and was never around very many people. To this day, he is shy and runs from anyone he doesn't know. Duster can have a very demanding meow, and he uses it to let me know when it's time to feed him. He loves to be rubbed on his stomach, and I know he's really content when the tip of his tongue shows. Duster spends a great deal of time outdoors and still enjoys sitting in the rain.

DUSTY "BC" SPANGLER
WAYNE, MICHIGAN

Dusty "BC" (for Bad Cat, of course) Spangler is a well-rounded individual in terms of size and personality. She comes when her name is called, and loves to be the center of attention, but she does not purr. She enjoys having her picture taken, sky-diving with her master, lurking in dark places, and, not to forget, riding in the golf carts at the local golf course. As you can see, Dusty gets around. She is most famous for the love bites she gives to her favorite people. And that's my cat Dusty!

EDDIE ("EDJU") DRAGICH
PITTSBURGH, PENNSYLVANIA

E ddie is a five-year-old gray tabby cat. His favorite hobbies are mole hunting, playing hit-taggers, and lounging on the back patio with all the neighborhood cats. He demands the finest in cuisine, including tuna in springwater. He will drink water only if it's in a separate location from his food, and milk only from a paper plate. Eddie loves his belly rubbed vigorously, especially upon greeting; loves to howl outside the shower; loves to bat the sink water; but most of all, loves to sleep leg over leg with his owner.

ELIZABETH CUNNING
ENDICOTT, NEW YORK

My cat's name is Elizabeth. She is a seven-year-old Himalayan with bright blue eyes and a beautiful beige coat. She is very attached to me and will follow me from room to room. Her favorite food is butter, which she begs for by staring and licking her lips. Lizzy is an indoor cat but is allowed on the front step when it is warm. If she hears a loud noise, or if someone approaches, she disappears back inside. She is very timid and allows only me to pick her up.

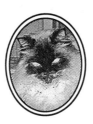

ELSA MARIE IMPERATO
EAST LANSDOWNE, PENNSYLVANIA

E lsa, an orange marmalade cat named after the lioness in *Born Free,* came to live amidst four children, a crazed Irish Setter, and a territorial gray cat. Needless to say, this experience "traumatized" him (a male cat named for a lioness didn't help, either), and today he is the epitome of the "fraidy cat," although he is totally devoted to his children. Born in the early spring of 1977 and orphaned with his litter, Elsa now is the chief pet of the family, and despite his innate shyness he is a friend to the children who grew up with him as their furry "crib mate."

ELVIS BOFF
FORT LAUDERDALE, FLORIDA

Now three years old, Elvis was adopted from the local humane society at age six months. A very affectionate black-and-white domestic shorthair, he loves to sit in your lap and listen to your voice. He is always purring. His favorite activities include playing with his favorite stuffed mouse and watching his own bird and lizard videos. He also enjoys a bowl of cantaloupe after his dinner every night. He believes he is human. Elvis is truly the apple of his owner's eye.

ESMERALDA HANSSEN
OSLO, NORWAY

E smeralda is similar to her son Mitchell in coloring and fur quality, though more delicate and feminine both physically and temperamentally. She was very good with her kittens for the first two months but has since sworn off motherhood completely. She avoids Mitchell whenever possible and has not yet given up hope that he will one day find his own diggings. The vacuum cleaner and "company" are the only other disturbing elements in an otherwise peaceful existence.

ESTHER (LADY GALLINA) GIUNTOLI
SEYMOUR, CONNECTICUT

Estee is a loving stray cat who came into my life five years ago. She's extremely affectionate and loyal, and one of the smartest felines I know. She loves to sit in the sun and smell flowers. She earned the name Gallina (Spanish for chicken) because she sits like a chicken atop her eggs. And because she's always the perfect lady, her daddy calls her Lady Gallina. Estee is also a loving surrogate mother to our younger cat, Stanley. My husband and I love Esther with all our hearts.

ETHEL IRENE GAY
DENVER, COLORADO

Ethel, a thirteen-pound gray tabby cat, was born in Annapolis, Maryland, on April 25, 1989. She was adopted at two months of age by Matt and Lisa Gay and moved with them to Colorado in 1992. Ethel is known for her constant dieting. In 1991, she lost one ounce! Playing catch with her dad, frolicking in the sun, and bathing her baby brother are just a few of her favorite pastimes. She dreams of producing and starring in her own feline exercise video entitled "Purr Those Pounds Off."

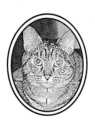

EULA ("OO-LA-LA") CAWLEY
UPPER MARLBORO, MARYLAND

Eula is a petite, polydactyl black cat, born in Ayden, North Carolina. She is the most vocal cat I've ever had the pleasure to live with. She greets me at the door talking a mile a minute, telling me all about her day, and does not stop until bedtime. She follows me around everywhere I go. She insists on sitting on my lap, no matter where I sit. She lives for being next to me. My husband has never seen me without my little black cat attached to me; therefore, I affectionately call her my "black growth." Eula is named after a psychic from the Edgar Cayce Foundation.

EVIL
SUNRISE, FLORIDA

Evil "Kitty" Opper, born September 5, 1986, in Florida, has black-and-white patches on her face that make it look like a skeleton's. Contrary to her name, she is the sweetest kitty in the world. She's real chubby and doesn't even mind if you use her for a pillow! She loves bird-watching, chasing lizards, and eating (her favorite food is chicken). In the morning, she likes to walk on my boyfriend's head until he feeds her. But when Evil just wants to relax, she lies right on you and goes to sleep. She's the most lovable kitty on earth!

FALSTAFF
CHICAGO, ILLINOIS

Named for being a big, good-natured klutz like the character in William Shakespeare's *Henry V*, Falstaff (the Nerd) is a large gray cat with white paws, nose, and chest. All four feet are declawed, and he's neutered. When he was adopted from the shelter, he came to live with the bossy black cat, Jekyll. To make matters worse, Clancy and Cayce, two other cats, joined the household. Now all three torment him. Of course, Falstaff doesn't understand this. We're sure he must feel, "I don't bother anyone and try to keep out of their way. Why do they abuse me so?"

FANNIE LEE MASSIE
EVANSVILLE, INDIANA

Fannie came into my life in a most unusual, scary way. It was reported that a cat had been seen in the outdoor lion exhibit. Being the zookeeper for the lions, I searched the area the following morning and found her holed up in a drain pipe. Fannie is a dark, longhaired, short-legged cat. She has pretty green eyes and a ruff around her neck. Fannie reminds me of a French can-can girl. She has a perky, flirting walk that accentuates her plump rear quarters. Fannie is my baby. She is a very affectionate cat that I love dearly.

FAT PATUTTI PRATT
NOBLEBORO, MAINE

Fats is a fifteen-pound tabby. Not exactly the friendliest cat, she lets you pat her once and will attack your hand on the second caress of her fat. She showed up on the doorstep eight years ago, meowing as if she knew who would take her in and love her. Besides cat food, she loves to eat plastic bags. When she hears plastic crunching, she comes running.

FELIX ("BAGGIE") BORTHWICK-MUNZER
WASHINGTON, D.C.

Felix is a thirteen-year-old, all-black cat who retired from street life at the age of three months. He lived for several years in Paris, where he learned his favorite French expression—*bon appétit*. His favorite activities are having his tummy petted, chasing (and retrieving!) foil balls and pistachio nuts, waking up his humans in the morning (too early), purring, and grooming his lifelong Siamese companion, Pooka. Felix firmly believes that there is nothing beyond his front door but the vet and the airport, and he disapproves of both.

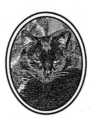

FELIX MARCHESE
SAN ANTONIO, TEXAS

Felix, a black smoke Persian, is a huge ball of fluff with bright amber-colored eyes. Like all two-year-olds, he can be quite playful at times, and he loves to go "cat-fishin" with Gene. When he's upset, he'll drag out all his toys and scatter them throughout the house, leaving one or two in his food dish. When really bored, he splashes all the water out of his water dish. He definitely has his own personality!

FERDINAND DE LUCCIA
NORTH HALEDON, NEW JERSEY

Ferdinand was a very large (twenty-eight-pound) tiger cat with gray and black stripes. He received his name because he always took our flower arrangements apart and then would walk all around the house with the flowers in his mouth—like Ferdinand the Bull. Ferdinand was extremely protective of his mistress and would attack like a dog to protect her. He was a very intelligent cat and could figure out how to open any and all doors. Ferdie always knew when his mistress was on her way home regardless of her schedule or the time of day.

FIDEL HODGES
BAKERSFIELD, CALIFORNIA

Fidel is a typical Siamese cat. He eats, sleeps, plays with a toy mouse, and gets high on catnip! During the cold months, he sits on the back of the recliner chair under the reading lamp to keep warm. Fidel is an indoor cat, but the dining room curtain is open for him to watch the neighborhood cats use the backyard as a shortcut. Fidel doesn't want to be petted, unless he's ready! When he's done giving you the privilege, he reaches around, bites your hand, hisses like the Exorcist, and waddles off!

FIGERO WAGNER
EVANSVILLE, INDIANA

Figero is a twenty-pound, half-Siamese and half-ordinary cat. He has big blue-violet eyes. He's been raised with dogs all his life, so I don't believe he knows he's not a dog. He comes to you when you call his name. When you hold him against your body, he puts his paws around your neck and actually hugs you. He plays on the back of the couch or on a chair seat under the dining room table. He gives a whole new meaning to having a cat.

FIREBIRD IMPERIAL COTTON
NEW YORK, NEW YORK

H e was born the morning of July 23, 1983. This beautiful Himalayan was named Firebird Imperial for his fiery red color and the Russian fable, a favorite ballet of his dancer mistress. And for his mother, Imperial Saki. It was purrrrr-fect love when he and Catharina met, and he came to live with her at just six weeks of age. Mischief is his game: snuggling amongst the silks in the lingerie chest, belly-flopping across the floor on his Bloomingdale's big brown bag, not to mention what great fun it is to play tackle with ankles passing by . . . OUCH!

FLETCHER CHORTOS
DEARBORN, MICHIGAN

Fletcher is a wonderful little stray who found me on July 24, 1987. He was very ill at the time, but after several trips to the vet his health was restored. He's a Morris look-alike, and equally talented, too! One of his many demanding meows sounds as though he's saying "Ma Ma." Although he weighs only nine pounds, Fletcher sounds like a herd of cattle as he races down the hall late at night. He loves his toys, owning over two hundred of them! His favorites are the furry mice. Fletcher is the PURRfect pet and doesn't get into anything.

FLUFFY ("BUTTHEAD") JACKSON
PLEASANT GROVE, UTAH

F luffy was the youngest in our family and typically spoiled rotten. Gray, fat, and independent, this feline had the life of a king. His favorite pastime, next to sleeping, consisted of sitting at the kitchen window watching the hummingbirds feed. He chased and retrieved aluminum foil balls and had regular attacks of the nighttime frenzies! Born August 20, 1987, he was a frightened little kitten when he first came to us. He brought joy and laughter into our home until we had to send him to "kitty heaven."

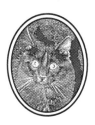

FLUFFY MIDNIGHT COX
DETROIT, MICHIGAN

Though not a purebred cat, Fluffy looks like a black Maine Coon. He has copper-colored eyes. We adopted him as a kitten on July 9, 1982, and celebrate his anniversary every year. He is a fat indoor cat who loves belly rubs, chin rubs, purring, jumping on my lap, warbling, kneading on me, sleeping, eating, playing with catnip toys, and posing for photographs when in the mood. When upset about something, he meows loudly. About two hours before each of his two meal times, he starts hitting me in the face with his paw.

FLUFFY ROYER
WHITEHALL, PENNSYLVANIA

Fluffy is part tiger and calico. She was at a pet store when I first saw her and fell in love with her. She was six weeks old when I bought her. She's affectionate, playful, and smart. She loves to "show off." Her favorite thing to play with is my rabbit collar. When she wants to play, she'll go in the drawer and get it out, then drop it at my feet so I'll throw it for her. Fluffy learned this all on her own. I never taught her to do that.

FOXRUN'S BLUE STARLIGHT
DAYTON, OHIO

S tar is a Blue Point Himalayan with a face that's melted more than one cat hater. He taught himself to play dead so people will jump out of their seats and he can lead them to the kitchen. Star judges people's IQs by how fast they can figure out he's fainting from hunger. He rewards smart people by turning his head up so they may kiss his cheek. Star's favorite games are racing to the top of the six-foot kitty playground (he's the undefeated Champion) and tricking his brother, Moonshine, out of the kitty maze.

FOXRUN'S MOONSHINE FLAME
DAYTON, OHIO

Moon is a Flame Point Himalayan, and flattery will get you everywhere with him. The only thing he likes better than being told he's beautiful is fish-and-fries from a fast-food restaurant, and he won't hesitate to stick his head in the bag to help himself. Moon likes cat food, too, as long as he thinks no one sees him eating out of a dish like a normal cat. He loves to play with his brother, Starlight, and even though he's usually outraced and outwitted, he only pouts about it part of the time.

FOXY KESSINGER
BOISE, IDAHO

Foxy is an all-black female with golden eyes and seven toes, which give the illusion that she is wearing mitts; she uses them like thumbs to snatch treats from my hand. She likes green vegetables and had to learn to eat cat food. She knows her name and the names of our other cats. She is friendly and stands upright on her hind legs to greet people—sometimes she'll walk a few steps that way. She sleeps on the foot of our bed, but if she gets cold, she comes up to me and wants *in*. She thinks she is "people"!

FRANGO FELLOWS
HOLMES BEACH, FLORIDA

F rango is a black tomcat with a sordid past. Rescued from a life of vagrancy and crime by the Animal Protection League, he still houses a BB in his tail and must have been quite the scrapper. His hunting days are over, however, and he only cheers his owners on when lizards and pests invade his home. We adopted Frango when he was four, and he's still playful at eleven. He is known for getting locked into cupboards and having to knock for freedom. He loves to sleep on his owner's pillow.

FRANKEN-CAT OSBORN
BROOMFIELD, COLORADO

Frankie is a calico female who got her name from the fact that her coat looks like she was stitched together with a Singer from various cat pieces-parts. She is the feistiest thing alive (although with less intensity since she was declawed and "fixed") and because she's only a year old we can look forward to many more happy years of having to put up with her. She is attitude incarnate—she sleeps where she pleases, she does what she wants when and where she wants to. In other words, she won't be confused with any of our four dogs or our other cat.

FREEBIE DUNIGAN CORDERO
LAS VEGAS, NEVADA

Freebie is a very spoiled Siamese mix with gorgeous blue eyes. Still very active at age twenty-one, he is in the process of training his third puppy, Suede. When Freebie goes outside, other cats don't mess with him—either because they respect their elders or because of his arrogant attitude. He has no teeth, but makes up for it with razor claws which he "sharpens" on his dog's face. Freebie is not very social or affectionate, but every night he tells his mom that he loves her by lying on her neck.

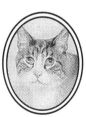

FRISBEE ("FRIZZ") SCOTT
WASHINGTON COURT HOUSE, OHIO

F risbee was never a *cat*; he was Marco Polo or Sir Edmund Hillary. His favorite "mountain" was the highest window in the barn, where he could survey his world. Getting there was fine, but getting down always involved a ladder and a friendly shoulder. Evening walks were a particular joy, but he always returned to his companion when his name was called, accompanied by a clap of hands. Frisbee is gone now, but his spirit will always be sitting in the highest window in the barn, free and happy. He is truly missed.

FRISKY SPILKA
VIRGINIA BEACH, VIRGINIA

Frisky is a black cat with white paws and a white belly. He has long hair and is very playful. He was found in Miami, Florida, when he climbed out of the pipes under the sink of a new apartment. Frisky now makes his home in Virginia Beach, where, even after being brought into a home with a dog, he has almost taken over. Frisky's favorite play-toy is a plastic spoon. He carries it everywhere. He loves to go outside and climb trees in the yard even though he has no front claws!

FRITZ ("ITTY BITTY FRITTY") STANDISH-SACKSON
NEW YORK CITY, NEW YORK

Fritz is a shy, caramel-striped kitty who resides on the Upper East Side. Being something of a recluse, he enjoys lazy days on the bed or a favorite chair and a very good meal. Occasionally he enjoys a wrestling bout with his older sister, Minuit, but he prefers daily contemplation on the joys of kittyhood. Fritz is five years old and was adopted from the New York ASPCA. Besides his sister Minuit, he shares his home with brother Punch, sister Judy, and his "people."

GAAZHAGENS MOLITOR
AMES, IOWA

Gaazhagens (Ojibwe for "cat," pronounced Gosh-a-genz) and his big brother Geist bring our manufactured home to life. Their intermittent *p-tump, p-tump, p-tump* down the hallway is a true pleasure . . . and so is seeing Gaazh, the lemur cat, sit up on his hind legs to get a better view. Gaazh's purring ways have rubbed off on Geist—you just look at Gaazh and he purrs, and now Geist warms up quickly, too. Each purrily stretches across a lap or shoulder of his choosing and loudly purrs outside the bedroom door at the sound of the alarm clock.

GABBY SPERANZA
CENTERVILLE, OHIO

G abby is a Lynx Point Siamese. She got her name from talking so much as a kitten; she's now seventeen and still talking! We've been through a lot together. We've lived on farms in the country, apartments in the city, a condo on the beach—and in three states. She had a leg broken in a trap, gave birth to kittens, and when one apartment building caught fire she escaped and was lost in the city "wilds" for three weeks! She really hates for me to go away, so when she sees the suitcase out she hides something I'll need.

GABRIELLE ST. CLOUD
(A.K.A. GABRIELLA, BRIDGET)
NEW YORK, NEW YORK

I got Gabrielle, a sweet/devilish gray kitty, to be my cat Zeke's friend and she loves him to pieces. He loves her, too, but she loves him more. She cleans him and initiates games of tag and surprise-pounce. If breakfast is late, she wakes me by knocking things off shelves or breathing in my face. Her voice, gravelly like a sheep's, gets regular use, for she loves to talk. Brave and tomboyish, she explores all noises, strangers, and unexpected occurrences. She's probably happiest sharing my sushi and cuddling with me in bed.

149

GADGET MORRIS
SPRINGFIELD, MISSOURI

Gadget is a light brown-and-white part-Manx cat. He's two and a half years old and very affectionate. Gadget likes to watch the birds and squirrels through the patio door. When he's cold, he sits on top of the microwave or the refrigerator, or burrows under the waterbed spread. He wakes up his owner, Toby, by jumping on her and patting her on the face with his paws. He likes listening to the radio and playing with his yo-yo.

GARFIELD "THE KID" KOLANOWSKI
HUNTINGTON BEACH, CALIFORNIA

Seven-year-old Garfield is the perennial athlete, accustomed to the spotlight, and a cut-up at parties. He quickly comes when called by name. Garfield loves to be held and cuddled when he's not sleeping curled up in a ball somewhere. His favorite toys are the cat pole that Robert built, small twist ties made into rings and pom-poms or "tweakies" that are used to play fetch and retrieve, and ping-pong balls. Garfield is a sable Burmese, gracefully muscular with a strong jaw and firm chin—a true lover!

GEIST MOLITOR
AMES, IOWA

Geist, named for the Scooby Doo ghost face of black dots on the back of his all-white head, is our stealth kitty. He's sleek yet muscular and one cool cat. Despite our efforts, Geist and his brother Gaazh insist on having the run of the house—slithering their way under the bathroom door on a whim. Thankfully he's easily provoked by his brother—they use up plentiful kitten energy on each other, leaving them happy to cuddle with us.

GEORGE HOGUE
BILOXI, MISSISSIPPI

George is a seventeen-year-old gray female cat with white markings. Half Blue Russian and Persian, she has been extremely active, but arthritis has slowed her pace some—after By-Pass surgery. George always accompanied me on my daily walks. Upon getting tired, I would carry her home. She's my companion and will not leave my side if I am ill. My husband chose her name, and most people think she is a male. George communicates with me by meowing constantly. She loves attention and is a beautiful pet. George has a sister called Muffin. They have been together seven years.

GEP ("GRAND DUKE") FRIEDMAN
NEW YORK, NEW YORK

Born June 21, 1991, Gep is a cat who's black all over except for a small patch of white on his breast. He loves to walk between your legs, and when he gets frisky, he kicks his hind legs like a rabbit. He really thinks he's a monkey and climbs our backs, and he'll sit on our shoulders like a parrot. When he wants attention, Gep sits in the middle of whatever it is we're doing and will *not* move until we talk to him.

GIGGLES THE CAT
KALOPA, HAWAII

Giggles is six years old, born of a pedigreed mother who was in the mood for a streetwise tabby. She has a full wardrobe, including a pair of bunny slippers and rainboots. She rides her Arabian horse, named Asian, and has mastered the art of cat-posting at the trot. She's a beach bunny, has her own Boogy Board, and swims well. She eats a lot of health foods, but she has a sweet tooth and enjoys cookies, chocolate, and ice cream. Giggles likes to snuggle with her kitty named Tarbaby after her bath. She's the best baby a mother could ever have!

GINGER BELLE LIVINGSTONE
DURHAM, NORTH CAROLINA

G inger was Alan's first Christmas present to Nancy, eleven years ago. She was rescued by Special Pals of Houston and came to the Livingstones. Shy, flea-infested, and scared, she took some time accepting her new owners—but once she did, absolutely no one else in the world could touch her. She adores her family, sleeps with them nightly, mostly on Nancy's arm, and has fits when her unacceptable cat companion, Vanilla, has kittens that invade her territory. Ginger has also lived in Houston, Kansas City, Los Angeles, Charlotte, and Greensboro. Despite her quirky personality, she is loved as a child.

less in 15 of

ee

24   Kelly Hrude
new   shots for the Sh
               Shanaha
               scored
Oct. 22   restored
disap-   two-goal
n the   45 sec
tion   the
ast   per
d   on
               a
ad   Yz
goal
games.   past
yed like specta-   from the left
we wanted to do   "Any time
night."   chances and
they did, much to going in, yo
rin of the Sharks, tle bit," Shar
ing the regular sea- think this was th
etroit since they came the least amou
               en I score a
Washington   Jose's

d.

case where it is
ear that this vest
what could have
y terrible tragedy,"
ohen, the mayor's
aff said shortly after
y morning shooting.

difference between a
fficer wearing his vest
able to walk out of the
l — really, within a
f hours ... and a police
ho is not wearing his
is either dead or has
he hospital and then
tion, is very, very
Cohen said.

words harken back
officer who police
ually scrupulous
g her bulletproof
n Philadel ia
Laureth

H
an
gloves.
crimina
police.

Hours afte
neighbors mil
cordoned-off c
Blood could be
ground, on the
and on the bottom
open door.

"The officer is
nate," Neal said. "H
spirits, he realizes
tainly God was on h

It is unclear wh
children witnessed
ing. Bob Ross, who
as a school aide, sa
bell would ha
when th

GINGER NEUMANN
LAS VEGAS, NEVADA

Ginger is the cutest bundle of fluff and fur. The way her gorgeous fur frames her face, she looks like a miniature lion. Ginger has a loud motor, and the happier she is, the louder she purrs. Her favorite way to sleep is to curl up under one of the bedcovers. Ginger loves being outdoors, and when she hears the door open, she runs inside with lightning speed. If any cat is in her way, she jumps right over them. One of Ginger's fun things to do is play inside a paper sack.

GIZMO BRIGHT
SNOW HILL, NORTH CAROLINA

G izmo is a black-and-white shorthair with two deformed front legs. The vet said, "Put her to sleep," but we couldn't do it. We had to give her a chance. That's why she became a house cat. She walks on her hind legs part of the time and jumps better than a rabbit! Sitting up, she looks like a miniature kangaroo and is adorable. She makes us laugh with her crazy antics. We gave Gizmo life and lots of love, and she gives us much enjoyment—even if she can be quite a little "Gremlin" at times.

GLADYS ABRAMS
COOPER CITY, FLORIDA

Gladys was born and raised in Boston, and loved to watch Larry Bird of the Boston Celtics play basketball on television. She was a matronly looking cat, a tabby weighing fourteen pounds. Her favorite activities included cleaning the bathroom tiles after completing her litter box routine, lying on the living room sofa for eight hours without moving, and sleeping between her owners all night long, gently whipping them with her thick, fuzzy tail. Gladys, we miss you.

GRAYSTOKE BURLEY
ELKRIDGE, MARYLAND

B aby Graystoke has sable-colored fur of medium length. His birthday is October of 1992. He learned the ropes quickly, since he has three siblings to teach him. Baby G. really likes to play the tissue game. You can throw just about anything he can carry in his mouth, and he'll bring it back to you. Baby Graystoke is a very handsome cat, and the personality that he's developing only shows his family that he is a wonderful gift that will always be cherished.

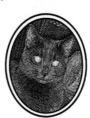

GREY GATSBY GELLER
BRANDON, FLORIDA

Gatsby, a fifteen-pound gray tabby, was adopted as a kitten into a Marine family. At age one, he was discharged into a retired Air Force family. He is strictly an indoor cat and loves windowsill napping. He has a fondness for perching on the banister, and likes to play ball and chase wadded-up paper. In the evening he has been known to run from a distant upstairs bedroom to the kitchen when he hears the cardboard lid being flipped off a carton of ice cream. His favorite treat is a dab of Ben & Jerry's brand. Do you think he's a spoiled feline?

GROUCHO IBE
SOUTH BEACH HAVEN, NEW JERSEY

G roucho is not your typical house cat. The full black mustache on his white face gives him the unique appearance of a miniature man. His multiple personalities vary between a soft, purring, lovable pussycat and a clawing, biting, hissing devil who easily takes the place of any first-class watchdog. He loves living at the beach, where he enjoys snoozing on the sunny decks and dreams of catching the sea gulls that fly all around him. He also enjoys long car trips to visit both his grandmas and family friends. Groucho knows Bruce and Laurette will always love him!

G.W. WILSON
LAS VEGAS, NEVADA

A gray-and-white shorthair with green eyes, G.W. is a cat who loves to be outdoors; if he's inside, he meows constantly until I open the door. He likes to sleep on the roof or in his own special "cubbyhole." If he hears someone arguing, G.W. goes up to each person and meows, waiting to be petted. That's his way of stopping the argument. One of his favorite toys is a ball made of aluminum foil that he rolls around. G.W. and another cat have fun chasing each other from room to room.

GYPSY LYSAUGHT
KANSAS CITY, KANSAS

Gypsy is an eight-year-old calico cat, adopted from the pound. She is mild-mannered until playtime, when the "wild" side comes out. She will chase me and bite my leg or hand till I tell her play is over. Gypsy naps on my lap as I watch TV, but if I try to take her off she'll meow in protest and bite once as a warning. She loves her pom-pom ball and can play alone for long periods. For attention she'll jump on my back unexpectedly, sometimes when I'm standing.

HARLEY DAVIDSON ERNST
MATAWAN, NEW JERSEY

H arley is fifteen years old and has long, soft, champagne-colored fur. He was diagnosed with diabetes seven years ago, and he hops onto my lap every morning without hesitation to be given his insulin injection. His age, illness, and the fact that he's declawed don't hold him back, though. He still manages to catch moles if we let him outside with us on a sunny afternoon. He's named Harley because of his loud and frequent purring, which sounds like a motorcycle. He also talks a lot and gives us more love than any other pet possibly could!

HARLEY JACK SKINNER
ANDERSON, INDIANA

Born October 9, 1990, Harley is a very spoiled Seal Point Himalayan. He was the only survivor of two litters totaling nine kittens. He insists that his bowls be topped off with fresh food at all times. He begs for treats day and night by falling down on the kitchen floor and putting all four feet in the air. He loves to play in his kitty condo, lie in the window, play hide-and-seek, and steal things that don't belong to him. He wakes everyone up at daybreak whether we're ready or not!

HAZEL SAMONEK
SYLVANIA, OHIO

Hazel is a longhaired, multicolored cat who was born in July 1986. She is friendly when she is alone at her home in Sylvania, Ohio. She will occasionally travel to Birmingham, Michigan, to visit her stepsisters, Marilyn and Maxine Johnstone. And while in Birmingham she really isn't amused about visiting. She will become very mean and spend her entire visit on top of the refrigerator, waiting until it's time to go home.

HEIDI ("PRECIOUS") GRUBBS
LYNN, INDIANA

Heidi is a Siamese/Maine Coon cat. She is ten years old and constantly referred to as a "pampered puss." She's fed on the kitchen table. She eats in one area of her dish, and when it develops a "hole" she meows until someone covers it up; if she has to, she goes and gets someone to do it. Absolutely nothing is allowed to be in her area of the table, and if something is there she'll meow until it's removed. Favorite activities are: eating catnip, lying in paper bags and boxes, and cracking my son's Legos.

HIDE-A-WAY HALL
CHAPEL HILL, NORTH CAROLINA

Heidi is the ruling animal in the Hall household. Although she's a cat, she thinks she's a dog. Heidi asserts herself by terrorizing all the other animals—she's not even intimidated by the two large Golden Retrievers. Unlike other cats, she comes when called, and trails along behind whenever her human charges go on woodsy walks. Totally self-absorbed, she'll pester you until she receives the attention she demands. There's no denying it—Heidi is the King of the Mountain.

HILLARY BREEN
SOUTHBURY, CONNECTICUT

Hillary is a fifteen-pound, orange-and-black cat with beautiful harlequin-like markings on her face. She was named after the mountain climber, Sir Edmund Hillary, because as a kitten she was always climbing—curtains, chairs, even people's bare legs! Hillary was a Father's Day present and has developed the habit of appearing in the bathroom while Dad is shaving because she likes to be rubbed with the electric shaver. She enjoys going outdoors and frequently returns with some sort of "prize" that she proudly deposits on the back porch step. Although she's not a lap cat, Hillary is loved by the entire family.

HOBBES MILLER
WASHINGTON, D.C.

Hobbes was named after his favorite cartoon character. As a young kitten, what he liked to do most was make his three law school roommates crazy! He still loves to scamper around the room, chasing the light of the flashlight (and becoming rather confused when it mysteriously disappears). He loves to play with his buddy Marshall, and his favorite lounging spot is across Deb's legs, where he sprawls out and purrs very loudly! Hobbes also loves to wake Deb up by sitting on her face and demanding to be fed.

HOBO MALOTT
BEREA, OHIO

In 1981, eight pounds of scraggly black-and-white feline tenacity literally lay siege and took possession of our home. On cold winter days, this cantankerous cat made pathetic "pusses" as he bathed in the heat escaping from our dryer vent. No one could enter the front door without stepping over the "welcome cat." Ultimately, this hobo catapulted into our hearts and home. He became a house cat the day he yawned and a hysterical damp sparrow flew out. Now, Hobie preens in the sun, perched on a bar stool, and specializes in decorating our home in Early Shredded Furniture.

HOGAN
SALT LAKE CITY, UTAH

Hogan is our hero. A blood donor and house cat for a veterinary hospital, he's a true life saver. Quite spoiled, he likes sitting in the mail tray to bask in the sunlight. His favorite foods include ice cream, yogurt, a daily dog biscuit, and anyone's lunch left sitting on the counter. Favorite pastimes include sitting out front on his leash tempting passersby to share yogurt, chasing things no one else can see, and tormenting helpless dogs. Hogan is a brown tabby cat with a belly that almost touches the floor. He's relatively contented, convinced he's the best, and loved by all.

HUMPHREY NIELSEN
EMERYVILLE, CALIFORNIA

Humphrey, a gray striped cat, was born April 1, 1981. In 1990 Humphrey, his two sisters (Collie/Black Labrador crosses), and I drove across the country to Boston, where I attended law school. On our drive east, Humphrey hid under the passenger seat, climbing out only if no cars were coming. We stayed in hotels at night (Humph was carried in and out in a pillowcase). On our drive back home, Humphrey (seasoned traveler he) stayed topside and viewed the scenery every day. His travels now are vicarious—he sniffs the dogs' fur for good smells when we come in from walks.

INDIGO HINCK (A.K.A. BOO, KITTY, BABES, INDU)
WORLAND, WYOMING

Indigo is a two-year-old Chocolate Blue Point Siamese mix. She is named for her deep indigo-colored eyes. Indigo is very shy because of the hard start in life she had. She was orphaned at birth and then raised in the animal experiment lab at Colorado University. Indigo was rescued by a vet and then adopted by her mom, Laura. Today, she is happy and adjusting well to life. She lets out loud meows and will whip her tail up and down very quickly when excited. But Indigo's most favorite thing to do is sit in her mom's lap and sleep or just be brushed!

INJUN KUBELDIS (A.K.A. SWEET PEA, CUTIE PIE)
HUNTINGTON BEACH, CALIFORNIA

The youngest of five, he's the ornery one of the bunch. Lazy, he loves to roll, stretch, and show how cute he is. His favorite game is to see how many cupboard doors he can open. After a bath, he'll lie or roll in the sun to dry instead of licking himself dry like other cats. Injun loves to be held and babied. He's very sensitive and is crushed when scolded or ignored. He can even make himself sick over it. Afterwards, he is spiteful. As a small kitten, he jumped all the way up into his master's arms. After climbing so high, he couldn't get down!

INKY BURTON
STERLING HEIGHTS, MICHIGAN

Inky came to us from a midsize college town. She's very independent and sociable, but on her own terms. If you're fortunate enough to have her grace your presence, you may be allowed to pick her up, but only until she's had enough. Inky eats her dry cat food from the bag it comes in and drinks water from the dripping bathtub. When she feels the need for a treat, she sits by the cupboard door and cries every time you walk by. Sometimes she's sly enough to get everyone in the house to give her a treat!

INKY DINK SHEELEY
PARK FALLS, WISCONSIN

Inky Dink is a small, sweet, shy, and dainty black-and-white cat who was found beneath an old abandoned clock shop. She also is sharp as a tack and impish! Whenever I roll her colored balls on the floor, she bats them back to me with the skill of a soccer player. She zips up and down her climbing trees in our apartment like a little monkey. And when she wants to play, she lets me know by bringing me one of her toy mice or a cloth flower. When I'm sick, she stays with me. She is truly special and precious to me!

IRISH SMARTMOUTH ROEDER
KINGSLAND, GEORGIA

I rish is a Siamese and American tom. He's an orange tiger color, only with longer ears. He got his name from meowing his answers, and spitting and hissing. His favorite sport is to sneak up on the dog and spit and hiss so the dog jumps. He loves to wander in the woods and the yard. His favorite place to sleep is in a paper bag.

ISADORA PEA ("THE SHORT CAT") REISNER
PHILADELPHIA, PENNSYLVANIA

A black-and-white shorthair with yellow eyes, Isadora Pea was born on October 1, 1990, and is a Philly native. She was adopted from a local refuge, singled out for her incage acrobatics (propelling herself across the cage on her back by gripping the bars with all four paws), and her goatee. Pea came with the name "Isadora" but was nicknamed Sweet Pea/The Short Cat because of her petite size and round shape; however, being black and white, she mostly resembles a black-eyed pea. Pea is a shameless flirt. Her favorite things include dog food (any kind) and wrestling.

ITTY BITTY KITTY
RAINELLE, WEST VIRGINIA

Itty Bitty Kitty (Itty Bit, for short) is a feline through and through. She has a son, Shadow, who is solid black, and of the two she's the typical cat—sleeping up high, hating dogs, and being a great stalker. She has a regal, above-it-all attitude that, coupled with fluffed white mane and arched back, makes her look as if she would feel at home perched—oh so delicately, of course—on a throne. Yet, with all her fluster, she will, after a long hunt, come scurrying in (escaping who knows what) and jump on my lap, glad to be home. In these rare moments, her blue eyes soften, and I think as she must think, "I am a purr-fect cat!"

181

JACK ESKALYO
BAY SHORE, NEW YORK

Jack is a six-year-old Maine Coon. He eats at least four times a day and loves to drink water out of the toilet bowl. His favorite spot is on the couch with his head hanging over the side. He's an indoor cat but occasionally sneaks out onto the kitchen porch to inspect the birds and bugs. He's very affectionate and likes to go to bed when you do—but watch out, he likes to nibble on your toes!

JADE ("BABY GIRL") PASCOE
TRAVERSE CITY, MICHIGAN

She's a sophisticated lady, and with huge eyes of jade she sports a stylish white fur! Adorned with a black masquerade mask and a black plume tail, she's a real heartbreaker and she knows it! On rare occasions we're even allowed to pet her, but never without permission. She tolerates her other two kitty housemates but would prefer to be an "only." She calls us loudly at midnight to invite a game of spongeball catch. She'll never tolerate even a speck of dirt on herself or a hair out of place. A romp in the grass? Her favorite escape!

JASPER ANDERSON (A.K.A. DUMMY-HEAD, RAT-FINK, POOKIE)

DENVER, COLORADO

Jasper is a pesky, inquisitive black-and-white shorthair. When he was a kitten, he was retrieved from a plastic bag in a garage in Michigan. He has a stuffed toy dog named Spud MacKenzie that he carries around by the throat. Jasper is very playful, and his favorite stunt is dashing through the house, kicking over his condo and crab-walking in a menacing manner. He loves sleeping on your lap, being carried around upside down, and sitting at the windows chattering at the birds. He always has a warm energetic welcome for everyone.

JAZZY MCCORMICK
MANHATTAN, NEW YORK

J azzy was adopted on March 10, 1992, from the ASPCA. Originally from Brooklyn, he was known there as Yogi Berra. White with a black tail and black spots along his back, Jazzy is noted for his exuberant personality and attention-seeking tactics, e.g., nipping at my feet and jumping on my back. He greets me every day at the door when I come home. Like an alarm clock, he wakes me at 5 A.M. for food. His favorite things: running, jumping, having his belly scratched, cuddling next to me, looking out the window, and playing hide-and-seek. A true great animal companion and friend.

JEFFREY-CAT
LONG BEACH, CALIFORNIA

J effrey was the only cat in the shelter crazily batting a ball around, and his playfulness won us over immediately. He was called Slim then, and although the name no longer applies he's still as playful as ever, eager to grab a passing shoelace or race into the nearest empty bag. But Jeffrey is a big baby, too, and will seek out the darkest corner of the closet whenever a noisy truck passes by or thunder rolls across the roof.

JEKYLL
CHICAGO, ILLINOIS

The black cat. The smart cat. The Top Cat. Found in the pouring rain at the age of four months, he's now ten years old and getting the gray hairs to prove it. Jekyll is not running out of steam, though. He's the head of the pride. His favorite hobbies, besides bossing everyone, are begging at the table (his parents are vegetarians, so this is really weird!), plopping himself down in the middle of the table when he knows he's not allowed there, talking back, and beating up on Falstaff when he thinks no one is looking. Jekyll is such a sweet cat!

JELLY CAT
SAN DIEGO, CALIFORNIA

J elly Cat is a three-month-old American long-hair with black fur and white markings. She was discarded in a large parking lot, and when found (at about two months old) she was tiny, forlorn, and starving. She was watching a mother cat with two kittens, and you could almost see her saying, "Why can't I be a part of that family?" After clearing her of fleas and worms, she became part of our family. She is very alert, adores our twenty-pound cat, and totally wears him down, notwithstanding her own three and a half pounds.

JENNIFER JANE FOULKE
LEWISTOWN, PENNSYLVANIA

Jennifer Jane is a mackerel-striped tabby cat. She and four siblings were found with eyes still closed and taken to Ronde Dalton's Kennel, where they were hand-fed and placed in good homes. JJ came to live with me after a year at the kennel. She had her own room, litter box, food, water, toys, numerous sleeping spots, and a window from which to observe the world. There she ran and ran around constantly. (Someday I must replace those curtains!) Now JJ has the run of the house. She loves to watch animals on the Discovery Channel from my lap.

JEREMIAH JASON JONES LEWIS
BROOKLYN, NEW YORK

Born in December of 1985, Jeremiah is a beautiful black, long, solid Burmese with exceptionally long nails. He's a peaceful cat, although he will attack when provoked. Like most domesticated cats in the city, he spends most of his time indoors; however, the apartment has a terrace that permits him a good run back and forth. He is selectively affectionate, and those whom he favors can expect to be nuzzled. Jerry has a daily battle with birds who land on the windowsill and flap their wings in a manner that seems deliberately to provoke him. His favorite snacks are cashews and popcorn.

190

JESSICA HORAN
DETROIT, MICHIGAN

J essie is a black-and-white tabby with a unique personality. Her hobbies include eating Doritos, chasing lizards, and attacking dogs of all sizes. She is known to be vindictive when ignored. As our attack cat, she has been caught attacking the mailman, gas man, and new neighbors. Despite her wild side, Jes is a lovable cat. She will greet you at the door and is the first to snuggle up to you when you feel bad. "One of a kind" is the only way to describe her.

JETTE STERGHOS
ST. PETERSBURG, FLORIDA

Jette is a beautiful smoky gray shorthair who is full of spunk and mischief. She serves as the family alarm clock by pushing open bedroom doors and loudly announcing each morning. Though an indoor cat without front claws, she recently protected her owners by capturing and killing a small snake that had entered the house through a screened porch.

JEZABELLE
FAYETTEVILLE, NORTH CAROLINA

J ez, our gray-and-white tabby, was a member of the family for eleven and one-half years. She was a well-traveled cat, starting out in New York and then on to New Mexico, Texas, and various areas of North Carolina. Jez was a nanny to my children, a very devoted caretaker. She was also very feisty and independent. We'll never forget the day she literally flew out our second-story apartment window to fight a cat who had been teasing her, not once, but twice in one day. Obviously, she forgot she was declawed. Jez won.

JIMMY ("LOUIE") DE LUCCIA
NORTH HALEDON, NEW JERSEY

Jimmy was a tiger cat with gray stripes and some white under his chin. His nose was like a bubble-nose because he had been kicked in the face when he was a stray. Despite having been abused, he was extremely friendly with people. Jimmy absolutely loved milk and had to have a dishful every day. He was a real clown and liked to do very unusual things. He had a special three-foot-long piece of clothesline that he dragged around the house like a security blanket. Jimmy's favorite position was on his back with his back feet over his head.

JOKER GEORGE NYMAN (A.K.A. BUNNY)
GARDNER, MASSACHUSETTS

Confiscated in a prison cell search as a kitten, Joker, now two, comes complete in a black-and-white uniform. Every morning we converse as he sits on the edge of the tub and peers through the hole he cut in the shower curtain. Evenings, he loves to share dinner; some of his favorite foods are chips, tomato sauce, and onions. At bedtime he takes sentry duty at the head of the bed. His favorite pastimes are napping inside plastic bags and emptying his toy basket.

JUANITA NICOLE BARROWS
HOPEDALE, MASSACHUSETTS

J uannie is a fourteen-year-old tortoiseshell cat. Since Christmas 1978, she has brought her family a lot of love and laughter. She reigns over the household from her throne atop the kitchen cabinets, quietly watching other animals and children, and staying out of the chaos! Her claims to fame are her vocabulary and a unique talent for balancing a beer can on her head. Juannie talks quite fluently as she mimics the person who is speaking to her and clearly answers questions we ask. She is also a terrific friend.

JUBILATION ITSY BITSY
MINNEAPOLIS, MINNESOTA

Bitsy is a sable Burmese. She is a "Blue Jean" cat now after becoming a Grand Champion Alter. She prefers home over the show scene. She is a real lap cat and likes to ride on a human shoulder around the house. She loves homemade tomato juice from the breakfast table.

JUBILATION WINCHESTER OF KIDEZE
MINNEAPOLIS, MINNESOTA

J ubilation Winchester is a Singapura (Alter), which is a shorthaired cat. He was shown for two years. He made his owner very proud by winning one National and two Regional awards in the American Cat Fanciers Association before retiring at the old age of three. He is very sweet, and when he sits up he always wraps his tail around his front feet.

JULIAN RAMBO PADGHAM (A.K.A. JULES, JULESESIS)
CARMEL-BY-THE-SEA, CALIFORNIA

J ulian Rambo, a five-year-old dark brown tabby, is quite a character. He sticks his rear end out the bathroom window to go potty on rainy days. Whenever a bully cat is around, he hides under his mistress's skirts or waits until his mistress or boy are close by before he'll hiss at it. His favorite place to sleep is inside his mistress's black lace leggings! He also sleeps inside pillowcases (with the pillows in them), bags of any sort (plastic, cloth, paper, whatever), and in the cast-iron frying pan on top of the kitchen stove!

KAYLA LYNN ROGERS
CHATHAM, MASSACHUSETTS

K ayla is a beautiful black longhair. She's eleven years old, and very loving and very spirited. She loves to play baseball and soccer with her best friend, Judy, who makes paper wads for their games. She's an indoor cat who loves to lie in the sun and watch the birds and the bugs, or in front of the fan on a hot summer day. She adores being petted but has no qualms about letting someone know she's had enough.

KENTUCKY ACCATATTA
PLAINSBORO, NEW JERSEY

Kentucky is a black-and-white tuxedo cat. He's my best friend and greets me at the door with a hug when I come home. He's always there when I need to talk to someone, seems to understand my different moods—and knows all I need is a hug. He loves to play, even though he's not a kitten. His favorite treat is a Pounce, and he will do all kinds of tricks to get me. He also loves unrolling the toilet paper.

KIKI CAT
HURLEY, MISSISSIPPI

Small but feisty, Kiki is very independent! She loves to chase mice and lizards. She also wants to get my birds and will often go right up next to the cage and stare at them. I can't leave a cupboard open or she'll go right on in. When it's time to go to bed, she won't come when called—she expects you to look for her. She loves tuna and milk.

KINKY
CHARLOTTE, NORTH CAROLINA

Kinky was a petite Seal Point Siamese, sharp as a whip. Once, when my electric blanket caught fire, she cried and carried on until I woke up. Another time we were preparing for company and she kept racing frantically up and down the hall; upon investigation, we found there was a major flood in the hallway. Yet another time, she raised cane about 2:30 A.M. by racing, leaping and howling; in the morning, we discovered our plants and stands had been stolen from our porch! Kinky also loved table hockey and was an ace player.

KITLEIGH SUE MILLER
AMERICAN FORK, UTAH

Kitleigh is half Siamese with bright blue eyes that glow red when she's upset and "the Siamese oozes out of her." She doesn't vocalize much, but she holds grudges and thinks she can communicate telepathically. Tired of being stared at with "voodoo eyes" when Kitleigh wanted to go out, her owner taught her to ring a jingle bell tied to the doorknob. But now Kitleigh prefers to stare at the bell, willing it to ring. Kit dominates any cat she meets but is reduced to a frightened, quivering mass by distant rumbles of thunder. She had nine large, healthy kittens in her first of three litters.

KITTY KINS DOE EVANS
SOUTH BURLINGTON, VERMONT

A beautiful black-and-white cat with gorgeous green eyes, Kitty Kins is a special girl and appreciative of the comforts of home—mostly because of her past of being a stray. She loves to be talked to while being brushed. We're close friends, so she's quite protective and always wants to be by my side, even while I'm in the tub. After all these years, she still gives me the "uh-oh" look when I get the nail clippers. I love her dearly like a child.

KITTY SCHUSTER (A.K.A. MOUSER, MISCHIEF, KITTY-FACE)
BOSTON, MASSACHUSETTS

Kitty Schuster, the Cutest Kitten on the Eastern Seaboard, resides with keeper Laurie. Kitty's exclusive birthday party is Boston's Event of the Season. Her trademark bow tie is *de rigueur* kitten chic. Hobbies are moth-catching and frolicking in the shower. She sleeps on her back, rear legs crossed in the air, front paws behind her head. Her day begins with a vigorous game of Nip the Keeper, awakening Laurie with toe, arm, and face nibbles. Kitty's goal is election to the House of Representatives. Supporters gather for her window perch appearances and chant her slogan: "Cats in House Keep Rats Out!"

KNOODLE BRASHER
NORTH POLE, ALASKA

I rescued Knoodle from the pound in August of 1991. She was four months old, a cute, playful kitten. She is still playful but is now up to fourteen pounds. Knoodle is a friendly cat. She always wants to be in the middle of things: my homework, the jigsaw puzzle, the newspaper, or any open box. Last year Knoodle won third place and People's Choice at the 1992 Alaska State Fair in Fairbanks. Knoodle is a house cat during the winter but spends her summers outside, chasing squirrels, dogs, and rabbits. Best of all, Knoodle cuddles with me at night.

KOTTE HINCK
CHEYENNE, WYOMING

Kotte is a one-year-old tiger cat. Her name means "tiger" in Sinhala. Kotte was adopted by her mom last year. When she first came to live at her mom's house, she was very skinny, but now she is very fat and happy! Kotte loves to prowl around the neighborhood in search of prey, her favorite being birds, which she carries home to show off proudly to her mom. Kotte also loves to play and chase her brother, Dudley. Kotte is now a happy and contented cat and very glad that her mom decided to adopt her!

KOUNTRYINIS BAMBI O'NEILL
FRAMINGHAM, MASSACHUSETTS

Bambi arrived by air from Independence, Missouri, in 1990 and it was love at first sight. He is a cream-colored mackerel tabby Manx, whose ancestors originally came from a lovely island off the coast of Ireland. Bambi enjoys riding around town perched in the back window of his owner's car. He has also traveled extensively by air and has received high praise on his beauty, intelligence, and behavior from flight attendants as well as passengers who observe him while prancing on his leash.

LADY "ASHLEY" GOODLOE
WHEAT RIDGE, COLORADO

L ady "Ashley" was rescued from an animal shelter in 1987. She was a very quiet cat and only stuck her paw through the cage to get my attention. She is a perfect cat and a good friend. Her favorite toys are large rubber bands and a feather toy. She loves dogs and hates other cats. Therefore, she assures that she'll be the only cat. She is a blue Russian and has won top honors at cat shows. She is a good friend.

LADY ESSIE GRAHAM
ATLANTA, GEORGIA

Lady Essie has traveled and lived in many places. A medium-haired, midnight-black Siamese, she enjoys her morning exercises with me. As I do my stretches, she will extend her paws gracefully in the air, follow my body movements, and exercise with me. During meditation, Essie sits quietly near me or places her paws on my chest and meditates with me. She has learned my moods and has become a friend to all people. And, though she likes to type while I'm on the computer, she needs to practice not erasing what I have written!

LADY SARAH OF BRENTWOOD
BRENTWOOD, TENNESSEE

Lady Sarah is solid white with gold eyes. She has a very regal manner, hence her name. She considers herself an outside cat but enjoys lounging on her master's drafting table and overseeing entries into the computer. The computer keyboard is always the latest model, since Sarah likes to chew on cords and is particularly fond of keyboard cords. Watching the plotter draft the drawings gives her great pleasure. Other happenings around the house get little attention from this feline, who is interested only in her own world.

LADY VANHEUSEN WHITE
WATERFORD, CONNECTICUT

Lady VanHeusen White is five years old and has black and white markings. She was born with only one eye, but that doesn't stop her from having an edge over her father, Conrad, who also lives in our home. Lady VanHeusen White, or Whitie, enjoys playing with her toys as well as anything we leave lying around. She loves to explore closets, cupboards, and empty boxes, and hides under the bed when company arrives. She is very special and likes to get attention from my husband as well as myself.

LAILA ("LULU BELLE") SIMONS
HOUSTON, TEXAS

1976–1993. Laila was a mostly Persian cat who spent nearly all her life in New Orleans. A true Southern belle, her favorite pastime was lolling about in Odalisque poses on surfaces carefully chosen to compliment her smoky black fur and huge green eyes. She was passionately fond of chicken, pizza, and potato chips. Rescued at an early age from the gutter, a tiny mudball, in the seventeen years thereafter she was never less than aristocratic. She spent her last years in Houston, surveying the world from the haven of a Victorian front porch.

LEON REDBONE ANTHONY
HOUSTON, TEXAS

Technically, he's an orange tabby, but watching him you'd think he was one of the dogs. They sleep on the waterbed together, beg for food side by side, groom each other, and play together. In fact, Leon's favorite thing is to wait until everyone's lying on the sofa watching TV, then come into the room with his ears back, his back arched, and slowly walk sideways till he gets someone's attention—then it's time to play tag as the dogs run in through the kitchen in a big circle.

LIBBY ("LIBBERS") DAVIS
ESCONDIDO, CALIFORNIA

L ibby is a small gray tabby cat. Her favorite thing is to play fetch with a multicolored toy fish with a bell on it. Anytime she wants to play, she'll bring the fish to me or my husband. Her second favorite thing is to crawl under the covers and sleep. She also loves pizza crust. On the rare occasion that I let her eat some, she works it off by running up and down the stairs late at night. When I wake up, she's always cuddled next to me and looks at me as if to say, "What took you so long?"

LILAS SPARKS ("BABY") KAY
CAMBRIDGE, ENGLAND

B orn on November 5, 1984, Baby is a rare Lilac Point Siamese cat whose two grandfathers were Grand Champions. He is extremely affectionate and will sit on his owner's lap all day—if so allowed. Apart from food, which he always tries to steal from his half-sister, Sweetie, he is beautifully behaved. His pedigree, registered with the Governing Council of the Cat Fancy of Great Britain, includes fifteen Champions.

LILY SCISSORPAWS KRENZ
LONG BEACH, CALIFORNIA

My wonderful cat, Lily, should actually have an entire book written about her. She is, after all, the most beautiful long-hair tabby around. And, as is to be expected, she has a winning personality. Who would have known two years ago that this little, undernourished, abandoned cat would become such a good friend and retriever? Corks are her favorite to fetch: within seconds, she returns with the cork firmly between her teeth (like a cigar). Lily also has a fondness for climbing the screen doors so the world can admire her lovely striped stomach.

LITTLE BLACK SPOT DORVAL
VERNON, CONNECTICUT

S potty is an eight-month-old, sleek, pure black cat with a scar across the bridge of his nose from Lord Spazz of the same realm. He loves to devour food of every kind, including sauerkraut and kielbasa. Human food is definitely more appealing to him than cat food. He also enjoys catching and eating insects like flies and June bugs. Spotty's favorite pastime is tipping over garbage cans. The humans whom he has part ownership of are James Courtney and Joely Dorval (whose pillow he enjoys sleeping on at night).

LITTLE BOY AMANTIA
MT. SINAI, NEW YORK

L ittle Boy, my twenty-pound cat, walked down our driveway in August 1987, thin, ragged, and hungry. I started feeding him, and though wary, he eventually came to trust me. We were hooked on each other by September. After a vet visit, he came inside. Puss and Kasey were not pleased but accepted him. L.B. is my companion and friend, the first on my lap; he sits on the table and watches me write or read. He sleeps in my bed all night under the covers, his head on the pillow. He's playful and opinionated, a real "personality." He is a special gift to me, I'm sure.

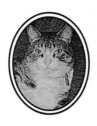

220

LITTLE JIMMY BERNSTEIN
BROWNWOOD, TEXAS

L ittle Jimmy appeared at the patio door on April 22, 1993, demanding food and attention. Jimmy is white and beige, and probably not more than seven months old. He looks Siamese, with rings around his tail and front legs. His eyes are bright blue and he just can't get enough love. He loves all other animals and people. He is not afraid of anything. His favorite thing is to put his front legs around my neck and hug. James is a fun cat to have around.

LITTLE MAMA JUDGE
GOOSE LAKE, IOWA

Little Mama is a tan, gray, and white five-year-old with big green eyes and a bright pink nose. She has this thing about licking the hair on your head. I swear she thinks it's dirty and only she can clean it! Her favorite game is "Hide under the throw rugs and jump out as you go by." Her favorite food is bologna, with egg yolk running a close second. She also requires sleeping under the covers with you at night. Little Mama is definitely a very, very spoiled cat!

LIVESTOCK MAGNIFICAT
SOUTH STRAFFORD, VERMONT

Master of gardens, slayer of mice, a nineteen-pound Maine Coon born in 1988 and raised in the home of George and Adele Benjamin (who miss him). Presently, Livestock is "Visiting Purr-fessor of Animal Linguistics" at Athens College in Greece, where he supervises the classes of his colleague Don Nielson. A seasoned traveler and car-lover, Livestock has recently begun exploring the Greek countryside in a Russian Lada in preparation for his forthcoming book: *Pondikia Polla (Many Mice)*. In this Orthodox country, he has developed a cult-like following among school and neighborhood children, who come on Sundays to visit "the little lion."

223

LOCKRIDGE'S SMOOTH SAILING ("JABBA THE HUT")
AGUA DULCE, CALIFORNIA

J abba is a six-year-old British Blue Shorthair. Almost human in many ways, he wins everyone's heart with his personality and unique face. He loves to go outdoors and roll around in the yard, but most of all he loves to work, and he is truly a ham. He has been in television movies such as *Lady Killer* and *Strays*. His big movies were *Pet Cemetary* and *Darkman*. Currently he is in cat food commercials on TV. Aside from work, he enjoys chasing his feline friend Chewy around the house and being the king of our Happy Home.

LOKI WALLACE
TUCSON, ARIZONA

L oki, a big black tomcat, and his brother Morris were born on April 1, 1977. Loki is nobody's fool when it comes to chow time. He will stand underfoot until fed and is known for his head "cock" as if to say, "Feed me, again!" He has even been known to howl in the hallway in the middle of the night when hunger pains arise. This starvation act was initiated at birth when he was fed milk from a bottle. Loki was also considered a great fisherman in his younger years.

LORD EATON HOFSHEIER
GOLDEN, COLORADO

L ord Eaton, now about three, arrived at the residence of Frank and Marianne Hofsheier, small, cold, and hungry, caring not that there was already a dog and cat in the house, only that he needed warmth and a good meal. His name evolved from watching him consume a great deal of nourishment: "Lord, is he eatin' again?" A gray-and-beige tabby with uncertain lineage (black Siamese-like legs, Siamese meow, Maine Coon fur tufts on his feet, and Persian fur), he has been a welcome scallywag. His favorite diversion is ripping hunks of toilet tissue from the roll and encouraging other destructive playtime with Paisley cat and Hannah dog.

LOUIS MASER
DURANGO, COLORADO

What is there to say about Louis, except that he is a most exceptional and distinguished lad? A three-year-old shorthair, Louis weighs in at about fifteen (or so) pounds. After acquiring him from the Humane Society, we soon knew this was not a normal cat. He is far too loving for a cat, eats tremendous amounts of food, and even attempts to bury any food he dislikes by a mock ritual of pawing the countertop near his dish. He loves to play-fight with Sadie, one of our dogs, and truly has the personality of Morris!

LT PIETROWICZ
FARMINGTON, CONNECTICUT

The very second we saw him, LT won our hearts. He is a real "talker" and makes his feelings very well known, especially around feeding time. He just *loves* his daddy, but Mom is nice to have around, too. He chases his sister all around the house. He loves to sleep on the windowsill and "sun worship"—he turns his belly up to the sun and will sleep there for hours. He also loves catnip and flips his body back and forth real fast so that he's covered from head to toe with it.

LUCINDA ("LUCKY") STORY
NEW WAVERLY, TEXAS

Saved from a near-death fight with a cruel tomcat, Lucinda was quite young when brought from a ditch into a warm home. Her coat is a glossy gray, and her flashlight eyes are an emerald color. Lucky's personality is a Dr. Jekyll and Mr. Hyde type. One moment, she'll be very sweet and affectionate; another, wild and running off to a solitary place. Usually, though, Lucky is very sweet and caring. She loves salmon-flavored treats and taking long naps in the sunshine.

LUCKY ("SPEARFOOT") COLLINS-TRACY

BENSALEM, PENNSYLVANIA

Lucky was found at Philadelphia Park Racetrack. He is easygoing and eager to please. Black with a white beard and pointy paws, he loves hunting birds and rabbits and socializing with our neighbors. Lucky is very good with his paws and is always trying to open the door or unscrew the lid on his food. He also comes when he's called and waits by the window for his dad, Tim, to come home at night. He had a brother, Tux, who passed away, and he still misses him very much. Lucky has a big heart.

LUCKY JUSTICE
NORTH ROYALTON, OHIO

Five-year-old Lucky is a real lover and the smallest of four cats in the house. He weighs fourteen pounds but is the baby. He lives with six Siberian huskies whom he gets along with just fine. When it's time to feed the dogs, he starts his meowing so you won't forget to feed him. He is always first in line for food—he has even had his head in the dish with the dogs. A junk food junkie, he loves potato chips and Fritos; when he hears a bag open, he comes running to get his chips.

LUCKY ("PSYCHO KITTY") SHAPIRO
BAYSIDE, NEW YORK

Lucky is a beautiful calico cat with multiple personalities. For the most part, she'd rather be looked at and not touched. She has a bad reputation with people, aside from immediate family members, as The Attack Cat. Lucky is as sweet as sugar with her favorite person and sleeps on his feet at night. Her other activities include destroying her cardboard-box cat condo and playing the gravity game with anything she can knock down. She enjoys resting on top of the cable-TV box and nestling in the corner of a closet.

LUCKY WEITZEL
WOODBRIDGE, VIRGINIA

Lucky is a tiny, three-year-old multicolored cat. She likes to chase our legs as we walk down the stairs. Lucky is a shy cat and often hides in the basement when people come over to visit. To keep warm, she enjoys sleeping on the furnace box. All in all, Lucky is a happy cat but wishes her teenage owner, Theresa, would pay more attention to her food dish and litter box.

LUCY IRENE GAY
DENVER, COLORADO

Lucy, a dark tortoiseshell cat, was born on March 25, 1989, in Annapolis, Maryland. The first of four feline children adopted by Matt and Lisa Gay, she is quick to remind her parents (and anyone else willing to listen to her constant hissing and growling) that she was once an only child. Lucy's hobbies include stealing pens and pencils, and taking bookmarks out of unfinished novels. She is developing a "how-to" book on assertive behavior that she hopes to market at cat shows across the country.

LUKE OWEN-SELLERS
JACKSONVILLE, FLORIDA

L uke believes that the Egyptians were right in worshiping cats. He is a blue-eyed Chocolate Point Siamese who commands attention by either jumping in your lap or nudging you with his head or paw. Most of his time is spent on the screened porch, but he also makes occasional trips around the yard to survey his territory. He insists on walking along the bulkhead by the water and has fallen in twice; he was rescued by his dad both times and is now affectionately known as "swimmer."

LULU DUBOIS
PALO ALTO, CALIFORNIA

L uLu is a longhaired black cat. She was given the name LuLu because she was so much larger than her littermates. Pam, her mom, thinks LuLu has vertigo because she straddles whatever she sits on. Her favorite spot is the wide arm of a chair, and when perched on it she resembles a gargoyle. She also likes to sit on the side of the bathtub and wait for you to throw a foil ball for her to retrieve; she'll bat it around the inside of the tub and then bring it back to you.

MAD MAXX
SOUTH PORTLAND, MAINE

Max is a Maine Coon cat. He is Kiera's cat, or maybe he's a dog. He isn't really sure. With his tiger stripes and white chest and paws, he's a very distinguished gentleman. He loves his dog, cucumbers, cantaloupe or most any other melon, and giving kisses. His favorite sport is nocturnal belly trampoline. He really builds up speed before he hits the target! (You.) Other than hanging out with Patty Paws, Cody, Kiera, Zackary, Jacoda, and us, he's got it pretty easy. He hates the outdoors but has been known to sunbathe on the steps if you hold his paw.

MADELYN CAITHLEEN PADGHAM (A.K.A. MADS, MADDY CAT)
CARMEL-BY-THE-SEA, CALIFORNIA

Madelyn Caithleen is a beautiful seven-year-old calico. She's Julian Rambo's mother. We call her Madame Crankles around the house because she's the "Boss Lady"! She is exceptionally intelligent and can open closed windows and closed doors, turn on bathroom faucets, etc. She also likes to sleep in cast-iron frying pans and is very devoted to "her boy." If she isn't kept inside, she follows him to school or wherever he's going!

MAGIC NEWMAN
WALNUT, CALIFORNIA

I'm the twin brother of Maximillion. We're totally jet-black, with sleek bodies, shiny fur, and the long, sculptured faces of Egyptian palace cats who once reposed at the feet of pharaohs. It chagrins Mommy that I'm the Great Black Hunter of the neighborhood. There isn't a lizard within two blocks that still has its tail, nor a bird that dares land in our yard. I'm loving when I feel like it, and my lyrical purr makes Mommy giggle and kiss me all the more.

MARMALADE BRENGEL
CHULA VISTA, CALIFORNIA

Marmy was born wild under my building at work. He was four months old when I caught and tamed him. He didn't meow for the first month I had him—now he never stops. He's been a sweet, loving member of my family for four years, although he still hides under the bed when friends visit. I'm not sure they believe me when I say I have a second cat, since they never see him. He is a big orange guy like Garfield and may be able to outeat him—his favorite snack food is popcorn! I'm glad he joined my family.

MARMALADE WHITE
DURHAM, NORTH CAROLINA

Marmalade is a towering orange kitty, standing about four feet high when reaching up a window. His head's a bit small relative to his body, and his vet remarked that he looks a bit like a tick. Well, of course he bit her. He weighed two and a quarter pounds at adoption. He went to a neurologist because he chased his tail so much, but there was nothing wrong with him, thank goodness. He likes to head-butt and will do it for hours. He's a bit stand-offish until you get to know him, but then there's no end to his depths. He seeks pen pals and will answer all letters.

MARY ELIZABETH WILSON (A.K.A. MARY BETH)
FULLERTON, CALIFORNIA

Three-year-old Mary Beth is feisty and fearless. A seven-pound tabby, she has no idea how small she is. Mary Beth is best described as your basic calculating "Boss Cat." She was a wild kitty we captured under a bush, apparently abandoned by her mother. This sweet little kitten grew into a miniature package of dynamite. She is very smart, very bossy, and quite a clever comedian. She is also lovable. Even if it has to be on her terms, she warms your heart and wins you over every time.

MATEO
WESTMINSTER, COLORADO

"Gruurow!" This whining growl of Mateo's is a sign of either satisfaction or frustration. An eleven-pound British Shorthair, Mateo speaks to us this way when playing "Slay the Spider," when he loses his ping-pong ball, or when he cannot get the blinds open. He also expresses his "Gruurow" when he's had enough of a vigorous back rub with a leftover cardboard wrapping paper roll. Mateo normally greets us at the door; however, if the maintenance man has been by, we can find this scaredy-cat huddled under the bedcover, and if you pet him while he's there, he'll say "Gruurow!"

MAX SHERF
SHERMAN OAKS, CALIFORNIA

This huge, huggable gray-red Persian with white choirboy collar and enormous white paws loves Mrs. Fields' chocolate-chip cookies. A watch cat, he guards the house nights against intruders and the whole western world from his daytime perch atop the chimney. He runs to alert you when the washer has turned off or a roast is burning, and sounds off loudly when you oversleep. But mostly, Max waits in the driveway until the end of the long workday and, as your car approaches, leaps up, somersaults, and meows in ecstasy for a kiss. He's better than a husband.

MAXMILLION ("MAXI") NEWMAN
WALNUT, CALIFORNIA

Magic and I were left in a box on Mommy's office doorstep and almost died from heatstroke before being found. We were five weeks old and looked just like little bats. Mommy already had lots of animals, so she took us to a shelter that supposedly didn't destroy animals. They took one look and said: "We'll keep them five days and then put them to sleep—who would want these ugly, gangly little kittens?" Mommy said, "I would!" and took us home. She adores us, and we feel the same about her. She tells us apart by our different-colored collars.

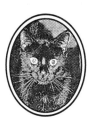

MAYA WILLIAMSON DIAZ
VACAVILLE, CALIFORNIA

Maya (named after one of my "sheroes," writer Maya Angelou) is half Siamese, two years old, and all black. An odd mixture of cat, dog, and person, she is spoiled rotten and knows it. She growls to warn us the moment anyone steps on our property, but then runs to hide under the comforter when the doorbell rings! And she's our personal exterminator—beware, bugs! Maya is also a well-traveled cat; she enjoys going on trips in the car and even helps drive sometimes! She has been many places—three states and Disneyland twice!

MEOW ("BUBBS") RAY
MARTINS FERRY, OHIO

Meow is a very sleek and sneaky Blue Point Siamese. Don't dare give him any love unless he wants it first. When we brought him home as a kitten from the flea market, we had no idea what we were in for. He knocks over the plants and puts things inside our shoes. Luckily, we found a way to get on his nerves, too. Get him with the squirt bottle! People who visit us say Meow has the wildest-looking eyes they've ever seen. When he meows, the sound is beyond words. That's how he got his name.

MEOW P. LINDSEY
WINFIELD, MISSOURI

Born December 9, 1989, Meow is a white shorthair with green eyes. She talks—and that makes her unique. Paper or plastic bags are her favorite toys. She wants fresh food, not anything left in the bowl over five minutes. She likes to wait for an open door so she can run outside, then sit and wait to be picked up. In the summertime, she wants to be carried around to smell all the roses. She's a bundle of love. Just having her and watching her play is a special joy. We love her dearly.

MEOWSER JARDINE HULL
MODESTO, CALIFORNIA

Meowser is quite a friendly fellow. Not only does he greet us at the door, but he also is very cordial to visitors—especially people who are allergic to cats. He's not a great sportsman, but he is an *avid* bird-watcher. He also enjoys gardening. He digs in the fresh soil, fertilizes it, and then, as everything starts blooming, he sprays—an excellent marksman! He's not much for TV but seems to enjoy the newspaper, plopping down on it just where you were reading. As he's getting older, he longs for retirement in the foothills and a little more shrimp.

MIA MARIE POWELL
EL PASO, TEXAS

Mia Marie, age eleven, is a black-and-white longhair with big round green eyes. She is very dainty and affectionate. One of the strangest things about Mia is that she enjoys baths, but only if the tub is *full* of water because she loves to wade around in it. She even drinks the water from time to time. Mia is also an admirer of music. She is that much more affectionate when she hears the violin, guitar, or the voice of singer Steve Perry from the rock group Journey. You might say she's versatile.

MIDNIGHT ("MIDDY-POOH") ATWOOD
PADUCAH, KENTUCKY

Midnight is a solid-black cat, sixteen years of age. She has a unique personality that makes her almost human. Her favorite toy is an old sock filled with catnip. Her favorite foods are banana nut muffins and "Little Debbie" fruit bars. Midnight is always purring. She loves to lie on the bed and be petted. Her favorite pastime is biting her mother, Michele (just in fun, of course)! She's an indoor cat and loves to follow her mother from room to room around the house. Sometimes she plays hide-and-seek!

MIKY WALKER
DANIEL, WYOMING

Born in New York State, Miky flew American Airlines to reach his new home in Wyoming. Miky is a Seal Point Ragdoll kitten. He weighed a full thirteen pounds at eight months, so he's going to be a *big* guy! His huge blue eyes don't miss a thing—from the smallest bug to the mule deer who visit his yard. He belongs to Fritz, a blind German Shepherd, and their games use up a great deal of his time and energy. Of course, plenty of pep remains for bounding through the deep pasture grass and climbing trees!

MIMI MACKOVICK
MINOT, NORTH DAKOTA

MiMi loves to play with strings, crumpled-up paper, and furry mouse-toys. She's the champion high jumper in the house. When resting, she loves to sit in windows and talk to the birds. Never at a loss for words, MiMi meows and chirps most of the time. She's an indoor cat but loves to try and sneak outside to chase bugs, leaves, and birds. Her favorite food is veal and whitefish. Her friend is Graucho, a puppy. MiMi is a year-old gold-and-white tabby. She's the best kitty I've ever had.

MIMO ("MEAW") DONOVAN
KENNER, LOUISIANA

Mimo is an English tabby given to the family about seven years ago. He is thirteen or fourteen years old. He was the first pet in the Donovan household. He takes a walk every afternoon with his Yorkie brother, Winston, and the neighborhood dogs come close to him and give him kisses. He is very happy to have Winston with him. He gets very sad when the family goes on vacation, unless he gets to go. Mimo is very particular with food. In the morning, he eats only hard cereal; in the afternoon, it has to be soft. He drinks water from the faucet.

MINDY McCARTHY-BOYD
DEVON, PENNSYLVANIA

Mindy, our thirteen-year-old silver tabby, is our official greeter and anyone visiting us must first say hello to her. She's in wonderful shape for her age, perhaps because she works out every morning with her master. (She does rollovers while he does sit-ups.) She relaxes the rest of the day until we get home from work. Then she's right at the door to greet the weary and, of course, to get her supper. She's very smart and knows our car when we arrive. She loves sitting on her deck in the summer; in winter, she lies by the fire to keep warm.

MINERVA HART
BRENTWOOD, TENNESSEE

Minnie was born on a farm in Tennessee. With her all-white body and gray tail, she was very cute. While she was a kitten, she wasn't very sociable. She would bite anyone that tried to pet her. Now, though, she loves attention and loves to be petted. Her favorite activities are chasing birds, spying on the dog next door, and lounging lazily in the grass. Minnie is fascinated with small animals and bubbles. She does not like catnip.

MING CMEJREK
ANN ARBOR, MICHIGAN

Ming was living at a cat rescue center when we found him. He was our first cat and made cat lovers of us right away! Ming is a Seal Point Siamese with beautiful blue eyes. He is extremely intelligent. He opens the cabinet to take out the can of treats he loves and opens the drawers beneath his friend Michelle's water bed so he can crawl in for a nap. When he wants something, he puts his forehead against ours and looks deeply into our eyes as if to say, "Read my mind"—or maybe he's reading ours!

MING TOY
SHOREHAM, NEW YORK

Ming was a Seal Point Siamese and mother of many, some of whom made their way into the lives of the Rich and Famous. She loved our old dog, Sarge, and would allow him to visit her new kittens. When Sarge was ill and dying, she lay on top of him to console him and keep him warm. Ming was also a bit too curious and found herself twenty-five miles from home via a repairman's van. It took her several weeks to get home. She was skinny and exhausted. Potato chips were her passion; no matter where she was, she could hear the bag being opened.

MINUIT ("BABOO") STANDISH-SACKSON
NEW YORK, NEW YORK

Minuit was found abandoned in upstate New York. She is an elegant sophisticate who enjoys lounging on the bed, the windowsill, or a comfortable chair. Her favorite pursuits include playing with her toys and an occasional wad of tissue paper or tinfoil. She also relishes fitting into an open shoe box for a well-deserved "cat nap." Minuit shares her Upper East Side home with her parents, brothers Fritz and Punch, sister Judy, and "baby" Nevin.

MINX ("MUNCHKIN") NYSTROM
DENVER, COLORADO

Minx is a beautiful gray longhair. As an indoor cat, she has made our home a giant playground. She wakes Mom for breakfast at six, turning her nose up if it isn't sprinkled with Parmesan cheese. Dad couldn't have made it through college without his study partner giving him some comic relief when he needed it. Minx has learned how to fetch and receives a full rubdown after every successful return. Her other favorite activities include riding in the laundry basket, doing laps around the house, and hissing at the big mean vacuum— when it's off, of course!

MISS AMANDA GUHL
JACOBSTOWN, NEW JERSEY

Miss Amanda, commonly called Mandy, is a small calico cat who's smart and affectionate and a great mouser. Born on a farm, she was given a loving home by Carol Ferrido. Mandy has many habits, which include hiding under the sheets and attacking intruding dogs. Recently, she went from being an indoor cat to an outdoor cat and has a great time when not competing for attention with Carol's other cat, Sparky. Carol and her son Kevin Guhl (whose name would have been Mandy if he'd been born a girl) still spend hours of joy with her.

MISS LILY GRAY
LAKE CHARLES, LOUISIANA

Upon hearing our cat's tongue-in-cheek name, "Mlle. Lily d'Allee Orpheline," folks are impressed. "Oh, a pedigreed cat!" they say. We explain, "No, just an orphan alley cat!" Recently Miss Lily's ten-year solo reign came to an end with the advent of a puppy named Key, a bit of fluff hardly bigger than a mouse. Nose out of joint, Lily treated him as such, cuffing him about unmercifully. Yet, watching Key mature, Miss Lily, never a mother and normally gentle and ladylike, apparently developed strong maternal instincts. Today, she tigerishly protects grown-up Key from bullying neighborhood dogs.

MISS MANDY FLEMING
SALEM, NEW HAMPSHIRE

Unlike her brother, Spot Fleming, Mandy is a little bit of a thing. She weighs in at around seven or eight pounds. All black, with a little patch of white on her tummy, she is quick and alert and an excellent hunter. Ants, mice, and birds must beware because she's awfully quick. When not hunting, she likes to relax by listening to some Madonna albums she has. Miss Mandy is also a very affectionate cat. She'll help you read the paper and then get rid of it by eating it. You might say she's really into journalism.

MISS PENNY SPRITE BOWEN
TULSA, OKLAHOMA

Penny, a six-year-old Flame Point Himalayan, helped start the "Cats Are Therapeutic Society" three years ago. She has volunteered 250 hours of pet therapy visitation. For her tireless efforts, she is renowned for being the first cat inducted into the Oklahoma Veterinarian Medical Association's "Pet Hall of Fame." Penny visits a nursing home at least once a week. The Bowens have three cats active in this visitation. Penny was *very* shy to begin with but she has progressed to sitting on laps and lying in bed with the residents. She enjoys her new friends as much as they look forward to her visits.

MISS POOGETTE ALLEN
BRIDGEWATER, NEW JERSEY

Miss Poogette is black and white with symmetrical features, including a black marking on her chin that creates a constant smile. Our little princess always wears a necklace of costume pearls and onyx. She is quite friendly and will greet all visitors with a rub. She will even rub on command. Miss Poogette loves to travel in the car and visit friends and family. She is never in a cage or on a leash. Our little girl is very intelligent and quite talented. She has even mastered opening her own can of treats.

MISSY KABZINSKI
TAYLORSVILLE, GEORGIA

Born July 22, 1984, in Macon, Georgia, Missy is half Siamese. Her face looks like the BMW logo. She has bright blue eyes and loves talking. In her younger days, Missy loved hunting and bringing her trophies home. Now she's a country cat, and it's easier to spend the day sleeping on her back in sunbeams and protecting the birds. As a kitten, Missy was cream-colored with light brown ears and tail. Each year God paints her darker and darker, and now she looks marbleized. A true best friend, full of life, love, and many kisses on the nose.

266

MISSY LESIAK
MT. PLEASANT, MICHIGAN

Missy, born in August of 1975, is a faithful friend. She has grown up with her mistress, a preschooler in 1975 and now a college graduate. Fortunately, she survived a fire at age ten after being given mouth-to-mouth resuscitation by the local fire chief. Missy loves to sleep, especially in the sun, by the heat vent in the bathroom, or under a light. Although she is elderly and still a "scaredy cat," she is queen of her domain, keeping George, the pesky neighbor cat, at bay. Missy is fond of popcorn, snack crackers, and tomato sauce. We all love her!

MISTY BLUE HICKERSON
HOUSTON, TEXAS

Misty is a beautiful Tortoiseshell Point Himalayan cat. When she was tiny, she had teardrop-shaped blue eyes, hence the name Misty Blue. Even though she is now fourteen years old, she still plays like a kitten. Misty has traveled around the world, lived in India, and for a time lived with me while I attended Vassar College. (She is sometimes referred to as "the cat who went to Vassar.") When I come home, she is usually waiting for me at the door, and the moment I sit down she jumps on my lap. She is a wonderful friend and companion.

MITCHELL HANSSEN
OSLO, NORWAY

Mitchell is a longhaired black, white, and gray kitten—Esmeralda's firstborn. He likes to eat—in particular, coalfish, cat yummies, bacon, shrimp, and ice cream. He never turns down a leaf or two of catnip. Mitchell spends his days snoozing, grooming, watching the birds, romping around, and waiting for dinner. After dinner and homemade ice cream, he usually relaxes with the family, snuggling up in somebody's lap or watching nature programs on TV.

MITTENS PIETROWICZ
FARMINGTON, CONNECTICUT

Without a doubt, Mittens is Mommy's girl. She's a beautiful tiger, and her greatest asset is her big expressive eyes—they're the first thing you notice when you look at her. She will only "talk" to us when we're outside and she's in the window. She loves catnip and does not stop rolling in it until she wears more than she eats. She is a very affectionate cat and loves to nap on Mom's lap. At night she sleeps on the floor on Mom's side of the bed, never too far away.

MITZY PRITZY COX
DETROIT, MICHIGAN

Mitzy Pritzy was born on January 20, 1984. Even though she is not a pure-bred, she looks a lot like a black Bombay with copper-colored eyes. She is a plump indoor cat. The normal things she loves are tummy rubs, sleeping, eating, purring, kneading, meowing, and, when nobody is looking, playing with a catnip toy. Then she has some abnormal habits that we do not like, which include licking plastic bags and eating cobwebs. She also likes to hit her father with her paw just before they are being served breakfast and dinner. Mitzy enjoys hitting humans, too.

MOET STEWART
VALLEJO, CALIFORNIA

Moet is an American Shorthair who weighs fifteen pounds. He loves to sleep in the sun and chase his twin sister, Chandon, around the house all night long. Moet's greatest adventure was the night he discovered the back door open. Most cats would love this, but he simply sat in the bushes too confused to cat about. Definitely a dog at heart, he answers to his name, will roll over, and loves to be scratched. His best friend and sleepmate has become two-year-old Kathleen.

MOJO SALVO
ARLINGTON, VIRGINIA

Mojo is a bad cat. She earns double warning signs posted on her cage at her vet's office. She loves soft, expensive food, which she washes down with toilet water. She belly dances, bites and scratches, and attacks fine wood furniture. Her favorite phrase is "I love you. No, I don't." She hates us. Yes, she does.

MOKIE BAIN
CRESTLINE, CALIFORNIA

Four-year-old Mokie is a smoky gray Russian Blue. He is an extremely loving and nosy cat. He jumps at the front door asking to go for a walk and is beside himself when he sees his collar and leash. He has his owner trained perfectly. I must sit on the left side of the couch with a pillow so he can lie curled in my arm. He likes yogurt, butter, and some cereals for treats—you have to watch your food! I would not trade him for the world.

MOLLY BORDIN
FOSTER CITY, CALIFORNIA

Molly is the littlest angel in her family. Although her heritage is unknown, her mien and demeanor are those of a princess. From the little white tuft of fur on her nose to the tip of her glossy black tail, she is royalty through and through. The sparkle in her eyes is due, in part, to the knowledge that she wandered into her rightful kingdom. She reigns over the kitchen sink with a graceful glance to all who would serve her. Her days are spent in the palatial luxury that befits her status.

MONKEY
LONG BEACH, CALIFORNIA

She's sleek and shorthaired, with a fine Egyptian profile and Cyd Charisse legs. She's a talkative cat, eager to let you know when she's ready to be fed or let out into the yard, and in her friskier days would pull the blankets off me in the morning to emphasize her point. Monkey is finicky and persistent, too, infuriatingly so! She'll perch only on the highest point of the furniture, and she'll not hesitate to ignore any litter box that doesn't meet her standards of cleanliness.

MOO GOO GAI PAN SHIRDEN (A.K.A. GOO, GOOBER)
WILMINGTON, OHIO

Moo Goo Gai Pan, born in the north Georgia mountains, is a beautiful blue-eyed Siamese. Goo was chosen partly because she was the runt, but more because she had singed eyelashes from sticking her face into a burning candle. (Her curiosity hasn't waned!) Goo lived in Atlanta for a year and then moved to Ohio. She survived an apartment fire while her people were at work and became front-page news by hiding with a fellow Siamese roommate in a closet. She thankfully was rescued once the flames were extinguished. Goo's favorite activity is loving her person!

MOOSE POTTER
MIDDLETOWN, RHODE ISLAND

Moose, a seventeen-pound brown tabby, arrived at the Robert Potter League for Animals in 1984. He decided to stay and was soon appointed Head Mascot for the privately run shelter. As such, his duties include animal-assisted therapy, educational advice, staff morale and supervision, and occasional kitten sitting. His dynamic personality shines in public relations. His weekly "Advice on Pets" newspaper column reaches 17,000 people, while his TV show, *Moose's Corner*, is viewed statewide. During his free time, he lounges on the reception desk or in various innovative spots around the shelter. He's a beloved, well-known community celebrity.

MORRIS HOWARD
ALEXANDRIA, VIRGINIA

M orris, an orange-and-white tabby, is a "one-man" cat—he lives only for his owner, Donald, and merely tolerates the rest of the human race. Born in New Jersey, raised in Manhattan, and transplanted to Virginia, he is still a city cat who prefers concrete under his feet. He does not meow but utters the sound "mer-mer," so he is affectionately called his owner's "mer-mer of the heart." Morris is a stand-up cat who never backs down from a fight with another cat or with any of his owner's unruly girlfriends.

MOUSE BILODEAU
JONQUIERE, QUEBEC, CANADA

Mouse is a misty-gray shorthair who, though shy and retiring by nature, will not abide anyone making decisions for him. While still a kitten, he chose Jean-Raymond "Bill" Bilodeau to be his valet, despite the fact that his victim was in the middle of a golf match and already served two other very demanding felines. Mouse was given to a friend, but he ignored food and lodging and took to the road. He caught up with his chosen master several days later on the same golf course, and they've been inseparable ever since.

MR. KEYS BATU
KEY LARGO, FLORIDA

M r. Batu, a Seal Point Siamese, lives on an island in a beachfront home. He allows his sister Rimau, a friend cat named Mandy Lou, two dogs, and two humans to share his home. Mr. Batu was awarded eight winning ribbons plus a Premiere designation in 1991. He enjoys a good game of soccerball but hopes to become a rocket scientist. Mr. Batu has never been out of the fabulous Florida Keys and—unless a hurricane threatens him—doesn't want to leave his island *ever*!

MR. SOUL
FT. LAUDERDALE, FLORIDA

Soulie, our black-and-white shorthair, was a son and "spitting image" of Zorro, the neighborhood Casanova. He liked to play with the hall mirror until the day Zorro attacked him—afterwards he seemed to think the mirror would attack, too. Growing in spurts (back legs, then front, back, then front. . . .), Soulie eventually reached a muscular fifteen pounds and took Zorro's place as the neighborhood terror. He used several of his nine lives in weird accidents and was one of the first cats to survive Florida's poison toads.

MR. WHISKERS RAYMOND
BROOKLYN HEIGHTS, NEW YORK

Mr. Whiskers was found in a parking lot when he was only a few weeks old. A gray-and-white shorthair, he got his name because a cocker spaniel that belonged to his original owner continued to chew on his whiskers every day (he permitted it) until he didn't have any left, on either his face or his brows.

Ms. Millie
CORONADO, CALIFORNIA

Millie is a fluffy orange longhair. I've never known a cat to be so affectionate, gentle, and good-natured. Millie has become buddies with our African Grey Parrot. Sometimes she'll go into the cage and take a nap. At night Millie always sleeps with my daughter, but at 5:30 A.M. she comes to my bedside. Her persistent meows and playful nudges wake me, and to the kitchen we head—me grumbling at her for waking me up, she chattering and dancing around with delight. Her favorite dish is Fisherman Stew. After breakfast she likes to slumber in the morning sunshine.

MS. SNOOPY
TAMPA, FLORIDA

One day in May, as I was walking across MTSU campus, out of a tree fell a calico kitten onto my hand. It was love at first scratch. Under the tree was a mama cat and kittens. That day Snoopy came home with me. Her favorite things include eating, sleeping, turning off answering machines, pulling kleenexes out of the box, unrolling paper, knocking phones off the hook, and being combed. She likes to smack you in the face with a wet paw or lick your ear while you're sleeping. At night she likes to sit in your lap, watch TV, or play with her toys.

MUCK-LUC FERGUSSON-DION
HULL, MASSACHUSETTS

Muck-luc Fergusson-Dion is an adorable black, gray, and brown kitty, Yankee born and bred. She amuses herself by popping up behind the sofa or chairs to scare people. To maintain her girlish figure, she plays hide-and-seek and participates in the Muck-luc Olympics with her favorite cat-sitters. The time of day she loves most is evening, when she puts on her harness and spends quality time on the front porch with her humans, Whitey and Babs, sniffing posies.

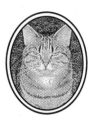

MUFFET MAE BOYES
GARDNER, MASSACHUSETTS

Muffet is a domestic longhair with tabby markings. At approximately four weeks of age she was hanging around a local prison, mooching food off the employees, and ultimately she found herself in a paper bag being lowered fifty feet out of a guard tower. (Today, four and a half years later, she's still afraid of paper bags.) Her favorite activities are nuzzling, playing, and sleeping in the sun. Muffet's favorite toys are rubber bands, string, jewelry, and bugs.

MUFFIN ("KISSY") GUILMART
DURHAM, NORTH CAROLINA

Muffin is a lazy fifteen-year-old longhair. Her muzzle, mouth, and stomach are white; her nose is pink with a brown spot in the middle. On her back are brown, black, and orange markings. Every now and then Muffin forgets she's an old woman and gets the evening crazies, howling as she speeds and skids across the wooden floors. When she's in an affectionate mood, she snuggles up close, puts her nose up to your face, and sniffs. That's how she earned her nickname.

MUFFIN HOGUE
BILOXI, MISSISSIPPI

A Siamese with beige and lilac markings, Muffin has beautiful deep blue eyes. She weighs nine pounds and will eat only Swanson chicken. When indoors, she walks throughout the house for thirty minutes, covering all corners of each room. She sits by the tub in my bathroom each night, and after bathing I have to rub her for fifteen minutes. She has a sister named George, and they have been together for nine years.

MUFFIN ("BAKER'S CHOICE") PUYA
BIRMINGHAM, ALABAMA

Born October 10, 1987, of Persian parents, Dueberry Muffin and Aldeeons Yankee Himself, Muffin weighs thirteen pounds and is one of the "Fat Cats" of Mountain Brook. He sleeps with his owner-mother, his blond head pushed close to her brunette one on the pillow. Muffin likes to drink ice water with a twist of lemon from a glass. He growls at dogs, strangers, and garbage trucks, but is afraid of a dust mop. Sleeping is his hobby, and he plans to "retire" one day in that big sandbox named Boca Raton, Florida.

MURPHY ("CAREER") BROGAN
DENVER, COLORADO

Murphy is a muscular black cat with long whiskers and two large fangs (eyeteeth) hanging over his bottom lip. When spoken to, he "chirps" in sentences to carry on his side of the conversation. His best friend is thirteen-year-old Benjamin, who is allowed to do anything to him in the name of playfulness. Murphy is known for his attitude—if he chooses to ignore your call, he will. He is subservient only to Diva, his kitty sister, who manipulates him to the hilt. His favorite activities include clawing furniture and perching on the windowsill to protect humanity.

MURPHY ("MIMI") FLYNN
WEST HAVEN, CONNECTICUT

Born in June of 1992, Murphy is our gray-and-white striped cat. She is not a lady. She attacks our miniature Schnauzer when he's not looking, climbs the wood paneling in our play-room, and slides down the first-floor banister (backwards). She knows we care, and every now and then we each get a turn with her lying on our laps. She loves to eat, play hard, and sleep on our beds, but her most favorite spot is my oldest daughter's bedroom. The toy she likes best is a piece of paper crinkled up into a ball.

MURPHY POTTER
MIDDLETOWN, RHODE ISLAND

Murphy, a Russian Blue, is second Mascot-in-Command at the Robert Potter League for Animals. He arrived there as a stray in 1983. Shunning the spotlight, he remains a behind-the-scenes cat, specializing in lunch patrol and dog kennel supervision. He is an expert doughnut and pizza box opener, as well as the self-appointed mouser for the property (a job he pursues with zeal, despite the discouragement of the human staff). Murphy keeps a contented purr ready for the asking, a quality that has endeared him to all who take the time to know him.

MUSTO HUMAN
JACKSONVILLE, FLORIDA

Musto is a portly cat who joined his human family ten years ago in New Jersey. He's been around, having resided in Maryland before moving to Jacksonville five years ago. A photo of Musto in front of his home was recently featured in *Jacksonville Magazine*. He is happily ensconced in his own little kingdom, where he regularly dines on baked chicken livers or filet mignon flown in from Atlanta. At Christmas he has his own tree of cat decorations. Considering the gourmet food, travel, and publicity, Musto is truly living the life (nine of them!) of the rich and famous.

MYNX ("PINKY") SCHPERO
ORANGE, CONNECTICUT

Pinky is a gray-and-white Manx. He was adopted by our family in 1988, and for the first three days we didn't see hide or hair of him. Pinky is unusually shy with new people and hides in a closet in the basement when he's scared. One of his favorite people is Baba Herbert. Since Baba has moved to Florida, however, Pinky is especially lonely. He has finally befriended Gil after almost five years, but with another baby on the way we suspect he'll be spending more time in his closet.

MYSSI BROECKER-HALL
VIRGINIA BEACH, VIRGINIA

Myssi was adopted off the streets and soon became mother to five kittens, two of which still live at home. A dark silver tabby, she weighs seven pounds and is very fast on her feet, especially when the front door opens. Myssi is one of the few cats that has to be walked like a dog. Her favorite sport is playing basketball with foam balls—she has thought of trying out for the NBA.

NICHOLAS DEER
ARLINGTON, VIRGINIA

Nicholas is a two-year-old Persian Coon, gray with large, dark stripes. He is shy and yet extremely affectionate. One of his favorite pastimes is bird-watching from his perch on the windowsill. The other is stretching out on top of the cockatiel cage and playfully tapping the birds within—until such time as they retaliate by nipping at his toes.

NIKKI RAYMOND
BROOKLYN HEIGHTS, NEW YORK

Nikki is a five-year-old, gray-and-white shorthair. She is a very affectionate cat. She likes to show her affection whenever you're sitting or lying down by climbing on your lap or lying on your chest while you sleep. She especially likes to become affectionate when it's ballplaying time and you're working at the dining room table, with all the paperwork spread out. Nikki then comes and lies right in the middle of everything!

NOODLEBRAIN POWELL
EL PASO, TEXAS

Eight-month-old Noodlebrain, named that because he acts so silly, is a white long-hair with grayish-black patches. He has a blanket that he stakes a serious claim to. He nurses on it, and whenever anyone tries to take it away, he lets them know with a fierce scream—as if to say, "Hands off! This blanket is mine!" He also lets everyone know when he's thirsty. He makes a whining howl because he wants someone to turn on the bathtub faucet to a trickle so he can drink from it. Sounds like a spoiled kid, huh?

NOODLES MCGRIFF
MONTCLAIR, NEW JERSEY

Noodles is a black cat who is very shy. He sleeps under the covers in bed with Bianca at night. One night Francesca, Bianca's sister, slept in Bianca's bed and Noodles kept hitting her to pet him. Noodles will only fall asleep if you pet him. Francesca didn't know that.

300

NOODLES RUSSELL JONES
DAYTON, OHIO

Noodles is a yellow tabby cat born in 1985. He was the runt of the litter and now he's the king of the house. Noodles weighs about thirteen pounds. He maintains his fine masculine body by eating both cat and human food (especially spaghetti), shedding pounds of cat hair daily, and getting plenty of exercise watching birds and squirrels. Noodles' favorite relatives include Kaboodle, who lives in Clarksville, Ohio, and Aunt Marcia and Uncle Keith, who live in Englewood. Noodles earns his keep by acting as security guard, alarm clock, entertainer, and stress reliever for the Jones family.

OLIVER WELLMAN-GLAVIANO
LAS VEGAS, NEVADA

Three-year-old Oliver is a gray-and-white cat with five toes on his front feet. He is declawed. He likes to climb fences and catch birds. If the cat food box or bag isn't open, he'll open it with his teeth at the tab or string on top; when there is only a little left in the bottom, he throws it in the air until it comes out. When he wants attention, he butts you with his head. Everytime Jimmie or Karen come to visit, he disappears just before they leave. He is afraid they are going to take him home with them.

OLLIE FIELDS
SANTA MONICA, CALIFORNIA

I stole Ollie from his mother when she was transporting her kittens from place to place. I didn't know this at the time. I only knew that a tiny kitten was meowing up a storm outside my window. I picked him up and brought him in. He fit in my palm, so tiny his eyes weren't even open. I bottle-fed him, litter trained him, and loved him. Now we call him "Fat Boy" (don't let him hear that). A four-year-old charcoal-gray male who can't stop eating. Oh well, he is a joy to behold, if you're able.

OOGIE FEDORCHAK
BENSALEM, PENNSYLVANIA

O ogie was the first of three cats to join our family. He is a nine-year-old Russian Blue who is true to the breed—often aloof, but demanding attention in the form of a friendly lap when he wants it. Eating and watching birds from his perch on our enclosed patio are his favorite activities. He studies people before befriending them, and the thoughtful expression in his beautiful green eyes leaves little doubt that a keen and intelligent mind lurks within. Naptime usually finds him atop some soft towels in the linen closet, which he can open easily.

OPAL KRUGER
REDWOOD CITY, CALIFORNIA

We adopted Opal from the pound when he was eight years old. He had been the only pet and had never been outside. He went into culture shock when we brought him home to our other ten cats and two dogs, but he's adjusted to them over the past three years. His favorite game is "Venus Fly Trap." He lies on his back all sprawled out and waits for someone to pet his belly. He then pulls his entire eighteen-pound body into a ball around your hand just like the flower.

OPIE KRENEK
IRVINE, CALIFORNIA

Opie, as you may have guessed,
Is a tabby, with orange-and-white
fur blessed.
A cat that talks a great deal
And follows commands like a dog . . .
   except for "heel."
A cat who owns the domicile
And allows her owners to hang out for a while.
His purr will knock your socks off.
He's been known to set the whole block off.
A cat who begs for "crunchies" and treats
As though the poor thing never gets anything
   to eat.
That's the story of Opie in a nutshell,
But if you were to tell *him* that, he'd give you
   . . . heck!

OREO DONNIE HENNEY
GILBERT, ARIZONA

Four-year-old Oreo is a black-and-white cat who likes to chase his tail and eat black and green olives. When he wants to go outside, he rings the bells that hang on our front door.

OSCAR LaNITE
ARVADA, COLORADO

Oscar, age sixteen years, is a black-and-gray tabby who loves to have his tummy rubbed. He has traveled through Colorado, Texas, New Mexico, and Arizona. He once had to live in the cab of a pickup truck for six weeks. He's almost toothless and eats twice a day. He has lived with black Labs and pit bulls. He is very quiet and gentle, and very much loved. I've saved all lost whiskers that I have found. He is a normal cat who does normal cat things. He has brought tremendous happiness to our family.

OZONE ("OZZIE") SCHPERO
ORANGE, CONNECTICUT

Ozzie is a black-and-white shorthair who was abandoned at my veterinary hospital after being hit by a car. His accident left him unable to walk in a straight line, and so he circles to the right. Ozzie has been with us for ten years. About five years ago, he slipped out the door and was missing for two days. We were distraught and made up posters and radio ads to find him. Ozzie found his way home unscathed. You can usually find him sleeping at the foot of Gil's or Molly and Jeff's bed.

OZZIE WILSON
FULLERTON, CALIFORNIA

O zzie, in a word, is a sweetheart. He's a four-year-old orange tabby with one speed: slow. He functions daily in one state: partially asleep. Ozzie's motto is "Why waste your energy doing it yourself when you can train people to do it for you?" His favorite things include stealing marshmallows from the dog, taking his rabbit fur mice to the kitchen one by one and whacking them under the refrigerator, and, last but not least, having his towel washed in Downy and changed two or three times a week. (It must pass the sniff test.)

PACO APONTE SUMMERS
MIAMI, FLORIDA

Paco is a talkative, lovable, lazy seventeen-pound tabby who sleeps on his back and comes running to a whistle! He adopted us as a street-smart kitten ten years ago and has proved himself to be an exceptional companion. He checks in with us every few minutes when he goes out to play and sleeps at the foot of our bed after he's lain on our pillow and purred us to sleep. If we awaken during the night, he patiently repeats his routine. When we go on vacation, Paco grudgingly checks into his sunny Miami hotel!

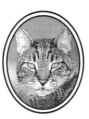

PAGE PEARSON
PLYMOUTH, MICHIGAN

P age joined our family on Halloween night of 1990. She appeared on our doorstep—this dirty, fuzzy black-and-white, flea-ridden furball of a kitten. Spooky! Page continues to live life on the wild side by *insisting* on being outdoors most of the day. She celebrates the sun with gusto by dashing up trees, shooting up onto the roof of the house, whipping across streets, and around and around she goes! She "talks" constantly, keeping us informed of her day's activities. She retires each night, exhausted, on our daughter's bed, dreaming her dreams. We love her.

PAISLEY HOFSHEIER
GOLDEN, COLORADO

The Webster Dictionary defines paisley as "a soft fabric made from wool and woven with a colorful and minutely detailed pattern." That describes Paisley, a ten-year-old calico belonging to Frank and Marianne Hofsheier. She and her five siblings were bottle-fed beginning at the age of one week, after the mother died. When she came to our house, it took several weeks of hand-feeding baby food and a great deal of TLC, but she survived to become a loving and affectionate member of the family. Favorite pastimes are biting Hannah dog on the back legs and cleaning her, and joining Lord Eaton cat in calamitous play.

PAMELITA CONCHITA ROSITA GONZALES
BROWNWOOD, TEXAS

Pamelita is a beautiful tortoiseshell born April 17, 1990, in Santa Fe, New Mexico. Her mother is a calico Persian; her father, an orange tabby. She has very quick reflexes and is an excellent hunter. When not out hunting, she naps outside under the azaleas or indoors in an antique Chinese wedding bed. Pamelita has a wonderful life!

PANDORA SUE CORONA
TUCSON, ARIZONA

Fifteen-year-old Pandora Sue is a black-and-white American Shorthair. She has certain peculiarities, such as refusing to eat cat food (probably thinks she's human) and sleeping on her mommy (me). She will not tolerate another animal on her property. She likes steak, chicken, fish, and chicken livers. She also enjoys helping you study or read the newspaper by sitting on the book or newspaper. She still goes out hunting and in the past has brought back such interesting items as a prairie dog (dead) and a snake (very much alive). Life with Pandora is very interesting.

PAOLO "SCAREDY CAT" GUIDOTTI
BOCA RATON, FLORIDA

Paolo is a living contradiction. He's a huge, twenty-two-pound, shorthaired black beauty, but afraid of everyone and anything that moves. He's not very affectionate, but *always* comes running to us for a friendly pat whenever he's called, even during his naps. A demanding fellow, he waits every morning at our bedroom door for my husband to wake up. Paolo immediately follows him into the bathroom, where he is then brushed thoroughly. If my husband is late getting up, Paolo becomes irritated, walks in circles, and meows loudly. You *have* to love a cat like that.

PATTY PAWS
SOUTH PORTLAND, MAINE

Patty was my first cat. She takes great pleasure in reminding me of that fact. We have added dogs, birds, and more cats, and her nose is still out of joint. Every once in a while, she forgets she's not speaking to me and she curls up in my lap and allows me to shower her with affection. Another little treat is to wake up with a little five-pound, black-and-white fur piece on your shoulder. Patty is notorious for her feet—she's all thumbs. We think she's beautiful. I hope she doesn't mind horses . . .

PAULO DYER
ROANOKE, VIRGINIA

Paulo is our foster pet, a petite cat who looks like a walking fur ball. She moved to another house in our subdivision, but periodically escapes and returns for a visit. Paulo learned to use the pet door almost immediately just by watching our cat, who took two weeks to train. She entertains our cat by chasing him all over the yard, nipping at his tail. If I want to pet her, she may humble herself and allow me one moment; then she'll hiss and run off to the man of the house, to whom she is loving, affectionate, and charming.

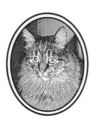

P.C. McNULTY-ASHCRAFT
APOLLO BEACH, FLORIDA

About three years ago, P.C. was rescued from being sold to a lab. His initials stand for Popsicle Cat, as when he was little he got stuck in the refrigerator for a short time. A black-and-white shorthair, P.C. is the father of two who also live with us. He's our resident thief, stealing vegetables, bread, and everything else left on the stove or counter. He eats anything, but his favorite foods are cornbread and asparagus.

PEACHES ("PEACHY") MASON
SAN RAMON, CALIFORNIA

Peaches was born and abandoned in July 1988. When she was adopted by Carolyn, Mark, Cyndie, and Scott, she could fit in a pocket and had to be fed with an eyedropper. She's a very petite orange-and-white tabby with green eyes, short hair, and a very long tail. She loves her family but glares, growls, and hisses at people she doesn't like. Her hobbies are: sleeping in sunspots, bird-watching, playing in the back-yard, attacking fingers and toes, playing with shoulder pads, and burrowing under bedspreads. She hates: other cats, being held, plastic bags, loud noises, veterinarians, and most people.

PEANUT ABRAMOVITZ
CLEMMONS, NORTH CAROLINA

Peanut is a self-assured, independent, but always affectionate eight-year-old tabby. Perhaps his greatest claim to fame is the extraordinary determination he exhibited as a tiny kitten, when he seized the end of a turkey drumstick bigger than he was and hung on for dear life! Peanut loves bird-watching, teasing his sister Chattel (a mixed-breed dog), and mood elevation via catnip. One of his favorite toys is a Super Ball, which he carries in his mouth; he allows it to drop down the stairs and then pounces wildly after it.

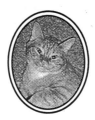

PEANUT SCHMIDT
EAST BETHANY, NEW YORK

Peanut stole my heart at the age of four weeks in August, 1990. "That runt is *so* ugly!" everyone said (except me!). She has grown into a beautiful tortoiseshell cat with perfectly round eyes. Strictly a homebody, Peanut likes to peer out windows (bird watching) or play hide-and-seek behind the sofa. She begs at the dinner table, especially for macaroni and cheese, cabbage and bread. Peanut is full of energy, playing floor hockey with a twist tie or wrapping her paws around my feet, tickling them when I'm not wearing shoes!

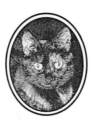

PEBBLES FRYBERGER
MOHNTON, PENNSYLVANIA

Six-year-old Pebbles is a tortie-colored short-hair. She got her name from the little tan markings on her coat, which look like little sand pebbles. Pebbles loves the outdoors, and her friends are the chipmunks. She plays with them and carries them in her mouth like little kittens but never eats them. She sits erect like a squirrel and can stand on her hind legs. She also chases the squirrels away from the bird feeders. Pebbles likes to play hide-and-seek under the pine trees. She loves to be brushed and combed, but not on her belly because it tickles.

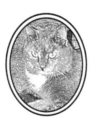

PEBBLES ROBBINS
EMMAUS, PENNSYLVANIA

Pebbles' favorite pastimes are eating and sleeping—neither of which has helped her maintain a slim physique. She has thus earned the nickname "Green-Eyed Meatloaf." In the rare moments when she chooses to be active, she derives great pleasure from chasing moths, playing soccer with paper wads, frenziedly shredding the toilet paper, and terrorizing her older sister, Raspberry. Despite her naughty tendencies, she remains the apple of her daddy's eye, and when she meows in that pipsqueak little whine of hers, Schw-eetie gobbles up *all* his attention!

PENELOPE-SUE OSBORN
BROOMFIELD, COLORADO

Penelope-Sue, a longhaired black cat with white highlights, can best be described as "elegant." Though sometimes confused with a humongous fat pear with batman-like ears and black fur all over it, she really is a cat—that is, except for the times she lets her composure slip and begs for attention by lying on her back like a big black puddle of fur until her tummy is rubbed and she's called a "pretty girl." Penny especially likes rubbing against the ankles of strange men and flirting until they make a fuss over her. Cat haters beware—this one even wore *me* down.

PEPO ("PEEPER") TAYLOR
PORTERVILLE, CALIFORNIA

Peeper is a large gray-and-white cat, with big green eyes, who since January 1988 has been the companion of Michele Taylor. A very picky creature, he will play only with toys made of real fur or leather, although one of his favorite playthings is his own tail. Peeper is an indoor cat but has a special windowsill in the bedroom from which he watches the outside world. If you're drinking water while he's around, you have to monitor your glass because he'd much rather drink yours than his.

PHOOTSIE ("FUZZBUTT") KIRCHBERG
AURORA, COLORADO

Born June 3, 1981, this gray-and-white long-hair mix (well mixed, we might add) descends from Tom Cat Kilborn and Fluffy (whereabouts unknown). Her favorite pastimes include eating, sleeping, and cowering under the bed during storms. Her peculiar habits are limited to lying on her back right where you plan to walk and licking holes in fuzzy blankets.

PICASSO DEPROSPO GLUCK
LANOKA HARBOR, NEW JERSEY

Picasso is a tabby with splashes of orange in her fur. She was adopted from a Martha's Vineyard shelter on Fourth of July weekend, 1988. She was only a few weeks old. Though an indoor cat, she loves to sit on the deck with me, watching the sea gulls and ducks. Her favorite pastimes include: riding on her "magic carpet," which I drag around the room; playing ice hockey in the sink with ice cubes; and playing "tag." Picasso actually comes when I call her. She's even mentioned in the book I wrote. There's no doubt that we love each other.

PIXIE
BALLWIN, MISSOURI

Our smoke calico cat, Pixie, is exceptionally affectionate for a feline and is always looking for an opportunity to jump onto our laps to be petted. She has determined that a prime occasion is when we are on the toilet. More than one startled guest has emerged from our bathroom after she has bestowed the honor on them! She also likes to wake me up in the morning with a "kiss," licking me on the mouth. Nothing gets me out of bed faster than fish breath at five A.M.

POCONO
WASHINGTON, D.C.

Pocono, born in the Pocono Mountains of Pennsylvania, is black with distinctive undermarkings in the shape of a perfect white bikini. Pokey is her nickname, which accurately describes her speed since she is twenty pounds of flab and fur. Diet foods don't seem to help. She makes an unmistakable "oof" sound when moving about, and as she looks up at you her neck seems to disappear. Pokey is extremely lovable and even has her very own adoring fan club with monthly photo mailings of Pokey being Pokey. Pokey say . . . I'm officially famous now.

POGO VARDAMAN
DAVIE, FLORIDA

One-year-old Pogo is a Himalayan cat who loves everyone. We should call him Shadow because he follows you wherever you go. One of his favorite pastimes is lying on his back when I play the piano and shaking his hind leg to the beat of the music. He also loves to watch me iron; he'll sit there motionless, watching every movement. His favorite toy is a rubber roller that he carries around the house like a prize catch. He is more to us than our pet. He is a good friend as well, and we love him.

POOCH YORDY
GROSSE POINTE, MICHIGAN

Pooch is a cutie of a calico cat, half of the sister/brother tag team Bowser and Pooch. She is best known for her: voracious appetite, getting under the covers, love of balloons, keen eyesight, "flopping over," courage and daring, and fluffiness. Pooch is very friendly but suffers from that deadly "I don't hear you" disease whenever being scolded. She and her brother have both been diagnosed with personality disorders due to the insensitivity of their owners in giving them "dog" names. Pooch is cute as all get-out! Pooch comes to a whistle!

POOH SCOTT (A.K.A. POOPS, POOPIE)
WATERBURY, VERMONT

Pooh, the only surviving quint born to my sister's cat in Massachusetts, is a beautiful steel-gray tiger cat. She's been a Vermonter since she was four months old. She does not like other cats and will defend her home fiercely, but the moment someone knocks on the door she's quickly upstairs hiding up on the closet shelf. Pooh can be very lovable, when it's her idea, and loves to stretch out and have her tummy rubbed. Her favorite resting place is the waterbed (she snores). She's a good mouser and occasionally brings me "presents."

POOKA BORTHWICK-MUNZER
WASHINGTON, D.C.

Pooka is a thirteen-year-old Siamese and professional lap cat. A former resident of Paris, she now understands such important communications as "Do you want to eat?" in both French and English. Her favorite activities are basking in the sun and surveying her domain from a window, cuddling up with her humans to go to sleep at night, and of course—since she's a Siamese—conversation. Pooka's humans are very well trained and know to keep her supplied with her own hot-water bottle and stadium blanket, which she's usually willing to share with her feline companion, Felix.

334

POOKA MAZUR
INDIANAPOLIS, INDIANA

Pooka is a domestic shorthair/Siamese mix, about six years old. She is the senior animal member of her household and spends a lot of her time looking upon antics of her cohabitants with indifference. She loves to sit in the windows for hours, watching birds flit by. She also enjoys occasional supervised visits outside, during which she eats as much grass as possible and rolls around on her back in the sunshine. At night she sleeps on the pillow above her owners' heads, purring and kneading.

POO POO WORKMAN
MADISON, TENNESSEE

Black with big gold eyes, Poo Poo has the voice and walk of his Siamese mother. He loves to be outside and loves to go for walks with us. As a baby he loved eating fruit, especially apples and cantaloupe. He expects a treat when he knows we've been shopping and always has to sleep in or on anything new that comes into his house. He enjoys being petted but doesn't like to be held tight. He gives kisses so we'll let him go. His favorite toy is a little catnip pillow.

POPCORN
BUELLTON, CALIFORNIA

Popcorn is a very small white cat with the palest blue eyes, born with a myriad of physical abnormalities of which he is totally unaware. He has an overabundance of toes on each paw, he's missing a tail, and his hips belong on a bunny instead of a cat (he hops instead of running cat-like). Our vet warned us he might not survive because he was missing some of the spinal muscles necessary for proper defecation. We prepared ourselves for the worst. Popcorn couldn't care less and continues to thrive, to play, to be the most mellow cat and to enjoy life as only a cat can.

POPPY LEE MAY
BOARDMAN, OHIO

My friend Poppy Lee, a Siamese, came to live with me three years ago. We own each other. Poppy watches out for me by telling me the doorbell is going to ring before it does and, at night, running from window to window if he hears strangers about. There is wonder, mystery, and magic in my friend. Poppy's bed is an antique bench with mattress, rose comforter, and his own green velvet pillow, yet his favorite place to sleep is the end of my bed. We play baseball every day. I pitch. He hits fencers, homers, one-basers, and out-of-the-park balls.

PORTNOY POLING
KINGSPORT, TENNESSEE

Portnoy is a golden-eyed, sandy-beige feline who never met a meal he didn't like. Being an indoor cat, his sources of amusement are somewhat limited, but he nevertheless makes the most of them! Watching TV upside down, drinking from the bathroom faucet, eating with his paws (the face-in-the-bowl method is sooooo crude!), tossing up killer fur balls, and lots of time devoted to love and affection usually manage to fill up his day. He is treasured beyond words!

POTATO WILLDEN
SALT LAKE CITY, UTAH

Potato was a stray cat we adopted after we found her injured near our home. As you might guess, she is very fat and lazy. Blind in one eye, she tends to bump her head on everything and takes a long time to jump up on something. Potato gets very moody if she does not have her food and talks to you to let you know you've forgotten her. She loves her milk rings, grass, and sunbathing in the buff. Tater has to be with you at all times, but only tolerates affection on special occasions.

PRECIOUS ("HELL CAT") CALLANDER
NEWARK, OHIO

P recious is a beautiful, solid-gray cat with gold eyes and a rotten disposition. She knows the entire world revolves around her wishes. She and her best buddy, Harry Wollins (the cat next door), smooch and hug every time they're together. Outside, they hide under the catnip and get high as a kite! Precious has a cushy life as she winters at her other home in Naples, Florida. She flies in the plane and the "stews" know and spoil her rotten. She is known as "The Contented Cat Who Flies Continental."

PREMIER FORCE MADAME CASEY'S ("PRECIOUS") LADY CHRISTY

EAST LANSING, MICHIGAN

Born April 19, 1989, Precious is a registered Tortie Point Himalayan. She has pretty blue eyes and a precious face. That's how she got her name. She loves to be pulled around the house in her red wagon, but she's so chubby that she hardly fits in it. She started cat shows when she was six months old. At age two she premiered after two shows. She loves my mom and follows her all over. She also fetches paper balls so she can have a treat. She is a spoiled baby, but we all love her.

PREMIER SIR NOGGINS ("MIDNIGHT") SATIN CHRISTY

EAST LANSING, MICHIGAN

Born April 19, 1987, Midnight is a registered black Persian with very large copper eyes. He premiered in his first cat show and received fourth and fifth best cat at the show in his breed and was fifteenth in the United States. Unfortunately, he developed a terminal heart disease. They said he would live to be two. He is now six. Between medication and love, he is doing real well! When it's time for his medicine, he meows at the cupboard to remind us that it's time. He's a little miracle, and we all love him very much.

PRETTY BOY BAXTER CAMPBELL I OF HAWAIIAN SNOWCATS
BATH, INDIANA

Baxter is a registered Persian white with blue eyes. He is very large but he is also very shy. He generally lies around on his kitty condo, but he also likes to sit in the window and watch the birds in the trees. Baxter is not allowed outside to play but finds plenty of mischief in the house. His favorite activities include playing with his toys and having his back rubbed. His least favorite activities include getting a bath, going to the vet, and having his hair combed.

PRINCE SMITH
BURLINGTON, NORTH CAROLINA

Prince greets me when I drive into my carport by running alongside my car door until I stop. One night he changed his routine and ran slowly in front of the car with his bushy tail straight up in the air. This had never happened before. When he arrived at the spot where I normally step out, he moved to the side wall and jumped at what I thought was a huge rat. It was a copperhead snake. It struck at him twice with force. My helpful neighbor killed the snake. Thank you, Prince, for warning me of danger.

PRINCESS ALVERS
NEW YORK, NEW YORK

P rincess is a kitty from heaven. She is black and white with a pixie face. She was found in a hollowed-out tree by our housekeeper in New Windsor. My daughter took her, and she lives in New York City. She is the office cat and the official greeter, jumping up on the counter to meet the delivery people. Princess is mesmerized by the fax machine and all the bells and whistles of the busy office. On weekends, she gets to come back to visit her roots and be with her country-cousin cats, play outside, and climb trees.

PRINCESS LANTZKY-BLOOMER
COLUMBIA, MARYLAND

P rincess was born October 1, 1969, under a barracks at Fort Dix, New Jersey. I have had her since that day. She has traveled up and down the East Coast and now for the last fifteen years resides in Columbia. My family loves her dearly, and though deaf she is still very healthy and alert. Because of her age she doesn't jump on the TV anymore, but when she was younger she would—then fall asleep and usually proceed to fall right off. She has outlived my two huskies, who also lived to be rather old, and now she plays with our four-year-old schnauzer, occasionally.

PRINCESS SUMATRA BEAN (A.K.A. JUAN VALDEZ)
PHILADELPHIA, PENNSYLVANIA

Bean, a calico shorthair with green eyes, was found at a coffee roastery. It would seem she indulges in her namesake as she ricochets from first to third floor in pursuit of evil phantoms. Her most astonishing stunt is her breakfast-time kamikaze plunge from the second-floor landing to the first-floor sofa via our open stairway. Like a princess, Bean is very elegant and graceful in posture and personality; however, her ultimate obsession is the flushing of the commode, a preoccupation that unfortunately predisposes to a rather unladylike solicitation of all associated activities.

PRINCESS SWINGLEY
TAMPA, FLORIDA

Beautiful and loving, Princess is a part-Persian black cat with just a touch of white on her breast. She joined our household after being dropped in our neighborhood about six years ago. She and I share our home. She would truly rather be petted than eat and has a routine whereby she must be petted thoroughly before she'll eat a thing. She requests that all visitors pet her before they leave. She knows she is beautiful, and I often find her looking in a mirror. Her gentle disposition makes her a perfect companion. I hope she can say the same about me!

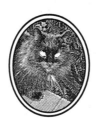

Princess Toots Lyndsie
NEWARK, OHIO

P rincess is an exceptional two-year-old. She is a great companion who is very verbal and very spoiled. She follows people from room to room and just flops down and waits. Before bedtime each night, she expects to hop on her special chair and ride to the dining room. She then puts her chin on the table and moves only her eyes while waiting for her treats. All day she sprints up and down the stairs, but at bedtime she is unable to climb the stairs and has to be carried to bed.

PRISSY PORIGOW
WINDHAM CENTER, PENNSYLVANIA

Sassy and lively, Prissy makes up in spirit what she lacks in size. During waking hours, she is a wildcat. When she sleeps or just wakes up, she is an innocent ball of cuddly fur that enjoys almost any position. If she wants to play . . . fine. If she wants to be left alone . . . watch out, she'll make you well aware! Her best friends are Squirrelly, Katie, and Alex. Her ultimate goal is to eat Izzy, the hamster she shares a house with. Prissy has a strange meow. Prissy is strange!

PUCK BERLIN
NEW YORK, NEW YORK

Not quite one year old, Puck is a gray-and-white-striped tabby with gorgeous green eyes. Puck was abandoned (in the company of his brother, Pepper) under a bush near the American Museum of Natural History, where they made history of their own by meowing loud enough to attract a group of passing dog walkers. Now pampered and petted, Puck has set his mission in life to investigate every nook and cranny in his new home, even if it means (and it usually does) dislodging whatever is in that space.

352

PUMPKIN SCHNEIDER
ALTAMONTE SPRINGS, FLORIDA

Pumpkin is a fat, happy, two-year-old calico whose favorite pastime (besides eating and sleeping) is to retrieve her toy mouse from the top of a high kitchen shelf. She grabs the toy in her mouth and then, "prrrowing" loudly (the way cats do when they've caught a live mouse), drops it at our feet. Then she waits for us to throw it back up on the shelf. She scrambles after it . . . and brings it back again. Pumpkin learned this game by herself and has trained us to join in the fun!

PUNKIN MEYER
WAYNE, ILLINOIS

Punkin was assisted into the world by Julie Yetman in November of 1987. He moved with Steve from Midland, Michigan, to Illinois in August of 1991. He dislikes car travel and tells you. Glad his college days are over, he has adjusted well to his new, relaxed life with his cat brother, Forbes, and his poodle brother, Buddy. He enjoys window-watching, sleeping in cabinets and on closet shelves, playing with sponge toys, and affectionately rubbing your nose. His distinctive purrs are as descriptive as words. Punkin is a timid, curious, sweet cat who loves attention (and gets it).

PUNKY RAY CARMINE BUBBA DEMARCO MILLER
NASHVILLE, TENNESSEE

Punky joined our family the day we saw him, a tiny kitten wandering all alone. He is now three years old, white with black markings, a black tail, and a very unique diamond-shaped brown mark on his nose. Punky loves to eat, sleep, and play—in that order. He also loves vegetables. Open a can of peas or beans and here he comes! He enjoys chasing backyard squirrels even though they're much too fast for him. Punky will even come in when his name is called. We love him!

PYWACKET ("PYE") DE LUCCIA
NORTH HALEDON, NEW JERSEY

Pywacket was a beautiful Norwegian Forest cat, and she absolutely loved being told just how beautiful she was. She was very agile, which was an asset living in a household with twelve other cats. On a run throughout the house, she sometimes would jump over and around four or five cats. Pywacket was very in tune with her mistress and always knew the type of day her mistress experienced. She always knew when a little pat with her furry paw was just what her owner needed.

QUAN LU
WARREN, INDIANA

Quan Lu is a spayed female Siamese cat who doesn't know she is a cat, having always lived with me in a one-person (widow) home. Occasionally she will slip outside, but all I have to do is prop my back door open and she will go around and come in. When I am resting evenings, she likes to sleep in my lap a few minutes and then goes to a carpet-padded windowsill. If she is unhappy about things, she can yowl a cry that frightens all who hear it. She is shades of tan to brown.

QUEENIE ROYER
WHITEHALL, PENNSYLVANIA

Queenie is a domestic shorthair with pretty gold eyes. She weighs twelve pounds and resembles a raccoon because of her size, tail, and black markings. Queenie is so affectionate. She is such a sweet and happy cat, considering she was abused, so I gave her the good and loving home she deserves. She loves dry food and all kinds of cat treats. And she loves to be held. Her two favorite places to sleep are on my dresser or with me on my bed. Queenie is a good cat too, because she never fights with any other of my cats.

QUINCY KING
AUSTIN, TEXAS

Quincy is an orange tabby kitten. When God was passing out the purr mechanisms, Quincy must have gotten three. He actually purrs while taking a flea bath. We aren't real sure how his personality will turn out, but so far he has been a wonderful and most enjoyable kitten.

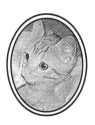

RACKETT LeCHAT
BARTLESVILLE, OKLAHOMA

Fourteen-year-old Rackett is larger than the average house cat, weighing seventeen pounds. He is rather a gourmet, enjoying the best of human food in addition to his cat food. In his younger days he was a wonderful hunter, bringing in through his cat door squirrels, mice, birds, and various insects—not all of which were dead. He is extremely affectionate and divides his time equally between all people present. He rewards attention, claw clipping, and brushing with a loud purr or cat talk, a meow.

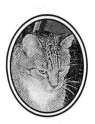

360

RAD ("RADICAL") CAT DONADIO
NARRAGANSETT, RHODE ISLAND

Rad Cat isn't just a cat—he's almost human. He is a two-year-old Siamese who is loved by everyone who has the pleasure of spending time with him. You are guaranteed some good "belly" laughs and amazement over what he is capable of. He loves his owner Nick—something like I've never seen with a cat. He actually plays hide-and-seek and also fetches. The best place he likes to be is draped around your shoulder and also sleeping under the electric blanket. He'll leap from the floor to your shoulder when you least expect it. He's the condo kitty of Narragansett.

RAFAEL GABLE PADGHAM
CARMEL-BY-THE-SEA, CALIFORNIA

R affie Gable is a huge, lovable blob of cat fur! I have yet to meet a person or animal who doesn't fall in love with this guy (even dogs like him!). He's mellow, friendly, and never stops purring. He eats just about anything, from cookies and cake to sardines. He's all white with huge gray splotches. On his cheeks are two beige dabs outlined with gray dots, forming a Clark Gable mustache. It makes him irresistible. Raffsters isn't as large as his housemate, Julian Rambo (who is twice the size of his mother, Madelyn), but his tummy is nearly twice as big.

RAFFERTY BORDIN
FOSTER CITY, CALIFORNIA

R afferty is a firstborn. As firstborn, he is Lord of his manor and King of his domain. Although he strikes terror in the hearts of his veterinarians, to all others he is a loving, if independent, fellow. He is an acrobat, comedian, and discriminating epicurean. His soccer skills rival Pelés'. Though averse to toll takers, he is generally an accomplished traveler. He has a mind of his own, though, and will let you know if the radio is too loud or the weather too inclement for his delicate taste. He is, indeed, a noble man.

RAGAMUFFIN SHELL
MORGANTON, NORTH CAROLINA

Ragamuffin was just that, a real mess, barely recognizable as a longhaired cat when she first appeared at our home. After weeks of feeding, she decided we were okay. A trip to the vet for bath and checkup revealed she'd soon be a mama. She had four adorable kittens who all found nice homes. She then made the decision to join our other cat and become an indoor member of the family. Just open a door now and Muffy runs the other way. She's living on easy street these days and loving it!

RALPH SWINGLEY
TAMPA, FLORIDA

R alph is a rather nondescript, very short-haired cat who came to my house looking for food about three years ago. He was frightened terribly of people. I already had a cat and so refused to feed him, thinking he would go away. After eight months he was still "hanging around." My neighbors convinced me to feed him: "Everyone thinks he's yours and he looks terrible." Ralph is very loyal and is still afraid of everyone except me. He now gets two good meals a day.

RAMBO BURDEN
NEW YORK, NEW YORK

orn August 25, 1988, Rambo really lives up to his macho movie star image: fearless flying leaps from ground zero onto his human's shoulders; bold and daring sneak pounces from behind, right on top of his unwitting senior cat, Bogart. Content to hide himself in the closet overnight, or snooze away the hours on his heated pet lounge, this happy-go-lucky kitty thrives on immature and bold escapades. His big green/blue eyes and sleek platinum coat add to his star-quality image. Those champion bloodlines from Entrechat cattery haven't hurt him one bit!

RAMONA YEAMANS
BROOKLYN, NEW YORK

"Ramona come closer, shut softly your watery eyes" is the full name of this slinking, emerald-eyed ebony feline, as she is the embodiment of the heartbreaking Dylan heroine. You'll make Ramona happy if you have long hair. Why? Her favorite playthings are braided ponytail holders of any color. After playing fetch with them for a few minutes, she hides them under the rug for safekeeping. Her special talent? She *jumps* really, really high. Photographic evidence exists of a five-foot leap for a tossed crumpled piece of paper.

367

RAMONA GERALDINE ZEZIMA
STAMFORD, CONNECTICUT

R amona is a four-year-old domestic house cat. She is small, sleek, and coal-black except for her white paws and whiskers and a white hourglass patch on her throat and chest. Ramona's greatest claim to fame is that she is even dumber than our goldfish, Pumpkin, out of whose bowl she likes to drink. A recent intelligence test pitting Ramona against a loaf of Wonder Bread proved inconclusive. She also is lazy, aloof, and virtually unemployable. Still, we all love her because, frankly, we are only human.

RASPBERRY ROBBINS
EMMAUS, PENNSYLVANIA

Four-year-old Raspberry is gray with two white toes on each paw. She is very attached to her mom and insanely jealous of anyone who diverts the latter's attention. Her most recent traumatizing experience was when her mom decided to marry "that guy who's been hanging around," which resulted in a move to Pebble's house (her new sister). She has taken solace in the backyard "jungle," where she can hone her hunting skills. (To date, her only catch has been a post-mortem bird from the attic!) She also escapes reality with a little help from the cat-nip bag.

RASTAFAREAN SPATS
HASTINGS-ON-HUDSON, NEW YORK

I found Rastafarean Spats in some local woods about ten years ago, when he was still a kitten. He's a black cat, with a white vest and white paws, but when his fur is brushed back he's totally white underneath. He responds best to the African "Clicking Sounds." Rastafarean Spats amazes passing joggers by rolling over and playfully outstretching his eager paw. And he "play fights" with an aggressive cousin, charging him with fierce determination, only to suddenly pull up, arch his back, and dance away.

RAVEN
FAYETTEVILLE, NORTH CAROLINA

Raven is a thirteen-pound black shorthair from Texas. According to her, she is our lead cat, responsible for law and order. Raven polices all activities that could possibly be interpreted as out of the ordinary. She is absolute Judge and Jury. Raven is also a big baby who loves to nurse earlobes. She'll snuggle in the nape of your neck and zap, she's latched onto your lobe. Raven also thinks she's the most gifted opera diva. She performs especially well in our large bathroom, howling until even the other cats smack her in the face.

REBECCA KREBS BARCKLEY
SALT LAKE CITY, UTAH

Rebecca is a midnight-black feline of innumerable talents and activities. She is a world-class houseplant destroyer and a relentless hunter of anything that moves. Her finicky refusal of almost any food has left her a complete tuna connoisseur. Becky is a loving companion, a tireless entertainer, and a constant, delightful friend.

REX ROST
ROUND ROCK, TEXAS

Rex is an orange tiger cat who came to live with us after my daughter Laura bought him at a pet store for seven dollars while she was away at school. He lived only a few short days in her dorm before he was discovered by dorm officials. He then moved in with us and became the most important member of our family. He is very spoiled. He sleeps in our bed with his head on my pillow, sits on my lap for toast in the morning, and loves to watch *Wheel of Fortune* from the top of the TV looking down.

RIFF RAFF PAGE
LAFAYETTE, LOUISIANA

Riff is a fifteen-pound tomcat. Most of his weight can be contributed to his super-long legs. He was born in March of 1988. Riff enjoys spending his time getting fresh air by the window, catching bugs, and, of course, catnapping. Riff is quite affectionate. When I'm sleeping, he crawls up beside me and plops down as close as he can get to me. Once I awakened to find him curled up beside me with his little paw around me, holding me. Everyone loves Riff. He's like no other feline I've ever seen.

RIP KING
AUSTIN, TEXAS

Rip is the head of the house. He is a fifteen-pound gray tabby and has just celebrated his second birthday. Rip loves all activities from ping-pong to playing chase. He has terrific paw/eye coordination. This is a cat even cat haters have to love! Rip loves to go outside on his leash. The cool concrete is his scratching post. The fireplace is his throne.

RIPPY
FLETCHER, NORTH CAROLINA

Rippy was a blotched tabby whom I adopted from the pound. He was a frisky little guy who was too young to be weaned. I taught him to drink from a bowl. Rippy was the typical curious cat. The toilet was a great fascination to him. He tried to figure out how he could use it until he fell in with the lid coming down to trap him inside. He loved to go with me in my VW bug. In the colder months, he wore his green sweater with matching hat. He propped himself on my shoulder and seat.

ROBIN WECKER
BOYNTON BEACH, FLORIDA

Robin, a Seal Point Siamese, was born on April 6, 1989. For her third birthday she was given a party. About 100 animal lovers attended. Robin enjoys music. When it's playing, she embraces the radio that sits on top of the refrigerator. She spends most of her waking hours every day on the screened-in twenty-by-thirty-foot "Robin's Nest" that was added to the house especially for her, watching lizards, birds, and anything that moves. She will play hide-and-seek, one of her favorite games, with anyone.

ROMEO DEPRES WOLFF
MIAMI, FLORIDA

R omeo, our four-year-old tabby, has just a stub for a tail. He likes to sit on the patio with his buddy, enjoying refreshments and treats (when he should be dieting). Romeo is part human (he snores) and part puppy (he begs for food), but mostly he is a lovable cat (hence the name Romeo). He loves to roll in his owner's workshoes and open closet doors when no one pays attention to him. He makes his owners forget their troubles with his comical characteristics, especially when he lies on his back with hind legs high in the air.

ROSE GAY
DENVER, COLORADO

Rosie, a single mother and survivor of kittenhood abuse, was abandoned by her former parents at age one. After a year of physical and emotional recovery at an SPCA in Annapolis, Maryland, Rosie was adopted by Matt and Lisa Gay in 1992. She is now a beautiful, well-adjusted, solid-white cat, living a life of luxury in the Rockies. Rosie enjoys sleeping in the linen closet, playing ball, and curling up on a good book. Negotiations are under way with several television networks interested in producing a miniseries about Rosie's story of survival.

ROSEBUD TALBOT
SPRINGVILLE, UTAH

Rosebud is a beautiful Persian kitten. He's the only kitten who is so spoiled that when he goes to the bathroom, I have to wipe his rear end. He's white, gray, and black. He loves to go for rides in our car. Ever since he was very small, when he gets hungry he'll come up to you, no matter what hour of the night, and bite your nose, or chin, or even your cheek. His owner is forty-two-year-old Linda Talbot. His favorite sport is to play with flies, catch them, and eat them.

ROSIE MEERSMAN
SILVIS, ILLINOIS

Rosie is a fourteen-year-old tabby, black, gray, and brown. She's very shy, but when in the mood she likes to be given a lot of attention. She enjoys sitting in a window in the fresh air, and when she gets her catnip she loves to just roll in it until she's covered with it. She likes to carry around her dad's socks, so if they're left out we find them just about anywhere in the house.

ROVER PORTZ
FAYETTEVILLE, NORTH CAROLINA

Rover, a black-and-white eighteen-pounder born in Berlin, Germany, was pretty much of a bully in his younger days and has already used several of his nine lives. He once fell from a fourth-floor window, and he has had to have surgery to remove a dime that he swallowed. He also lost a tooth in his sister Sissy Cat's collar. He loves to go outside, eat pizza, and sleep in the bedsprings. His special toy is a long-legged spider, which can often be found in his water or food bowl.

RUDOLPH WINSTON OBERG (A.K.A. POODIE)
WAYNESVILLE, NORTH CAROLINA

P oodie, a two-year-old marmalade exotic shorthair, was rescued from death row at the local animal shelter by the Obergs when he was six months old. His expressive face is a pug (Winston Churchill) with a tiny, red nose (Rudolph). Poodie is typical of exotics in that he demands attention, attempts to dominate the other three cats, and loves to love his master and mistress. His hobbies include stalking birds from the catnip bush, giving "purr-meow" wake-up calls each morning at six, sleeping in his antique Coca-Cola box, and "air paws." The Obergs adore their Poodie!

SABRINA ("WEENA") LEWIS
VILAS, NORTH CAROLINA

Sabrina, at thirteen and a half, is as sassy as ever. She commands respect and attention, and if not received on *her* demand, punishment is quickly received in the form of a growl. Upon entering the house at bedtime, she is asked, "Did you go to the bathroom?" If affirmative, she'll growl. If not, she says nothing. She owns Ed's lap, and Ed. She'll move in with Jean, sleeping on her legs, when the mood suits her. She also rules the Adams' dog, Penny. Despite arthritis and some excess pounds, she still manages to get into some rather strange sleeping positions!

SADIE LOU MCCONNELL
OCEANSIDE, CALIFORNIA

Sadie is a little brown Burmese. She was the runt of the litter, born May of 1991. She weighs only six pounds but is the boss! She loves crunchy things to eat, especially potato chips. Every time I go near the front door, she's there, yelling at me to take her with me. She loves riding in the car and insists on it every chance she gets! She sleeps under the covers and behind my knees at night. She likes to bite my nose—I think she thinks she's kissing me.

SAILOR MIGHTY HOLDEN
SHERMAN OAKS, CALIFORNIA

Born on March 13, 1991, in Palm Springs, California, Sailor Mighty Holden spent his first six weeks at a pet orphanage determined to find a better home. And boy did he! Sailor now shares a mini-estate with his adopted sister in a plush area of Los Angeles. He is a black-and-white tuxedo cat with a pink nose and hazel eyes. He is proud and he is loud, with a very inquisitive nature. Sailor's favorite activity is riding in the car. He loves to see the world around him. The word "impossible" is not in his vocabulary.

SALLY-ALICE SCOTT
RIVERSIDE, CALIFORNIA

With this unusual name, it's obvious that the family couldn't agree on which name suited her. Sally-Alice patiently endured having her nails clipped, her ears cleaned, baths, and repeated combings by a group of enthusiastic 4-H members of the Cat Project. But she was a star in other ways and enjoyed an illustrious career in the Household Pet show ring, always garnering a final win and a trophy at every show. Her affection for everyone and her ladylike behavior made her a favorite. Most important, she loved and was loved by all who knew her.

SAM KESSINGER
BOISE, IDAHO

Sam is an all-black cat, approximately thirteen years old. He came to our home when he was less than a year old and made himself at home with our other kitten. He comes when I whistle or call his name. Once reprimanded for catching a baby chicken, he thereafter volunteered to be their guardian. When a baby chick got out of the pen, he carried it back and set it down, unhurt, at my feet. When we had a sick chicken in a box in the house, Sam stayed right beside the box until the chicken was well. He would not let the other cats near.

SAMANTHA ANSELL
SALT LAKE CITY, UTAH

Samantha, our three-year-old calico Persian, is as mischievous as her large copper eyes. We knew that she would provide us with a lifetime of pleasure when we first went to meet her. She squatted over her littermates' dry food bowl, scratched a little hole, and did her business! Sam's markings are similar to Garfield's, but her demeanor is much more obstinate! Everything is on her terms: "You can pet me when it's all right with me" ... "Don't comb me; I like my fur matted" ... "I'll sleep on your head if I want to!"

389

SAMANTHA BELL
APPLETON, WISCONSIN

Sam is half Siamese but *all* Siamese personality and very spoiled. She is a beautiful cat, although she has a fat pouch that swings when she terrorizes the house. She is always waiting at the back door for us and actually loves to play fetch. Sam hates visitors and harasses them by hissing and growling at them. Her favorite activity is eating. If we don't get up immediately after the alarm sounds, she pounces on our bladders or darts across the back of our pillows and rattles the closet door until she gets her breakfast!

SAMANTHA KELLEY
LYNN, MASSACHUSETTS

Samantha is a six-year-old Maine Coon tabby. She had fifteen foster brothers and sisters. Now she's the only one left. Shy to strangers, especially men, her personality shines once her confidence is gained. She was brought up with Bo-Bo, a Labrador Retriever. Her pastimes are bird-watching, following TV sports, and visiting nursing homes. Samantha has appeared twice in the Boston *Herald* and twice in the Lynn *Daily Evening Item*. She can dance, serves breakfast, and models baby clothes. Samantha, you're O.K.!

SAM CAT WALLACE
POWAY, CALIFORNIA

He's big (twenty pounds), he's bad (just ask him!), and he's got huge green eyes. He's "King of the Corner" where he lives. In his nine-year reign, he's done a lot of napping—most often in the lap of one of his lucky owners. Since he's able to open the front and back screen doors, he travels quite freely. Once we lost him for three weeks. Apparently he got his fill of roaming that last time. Since returning, he has regained the weight he lost and is once more the big, beautiful tiger-striped "King of the Corner"!

SANDY COTTON
AUSTIN, TEXAS

L ittle Sandy was given to the Cottons in July 1979. She is their only Siamese who weighs a mere six pounds and has the prettiest blue eyes. She does have the Siamese cry, and if she wants something, you know about it. If you talk real sweet to her, she'll put her head down and stand on her back, toes so high she almost does a somersault. Even though all the Cottons' cats are neutered or spayed, Sandy has always been a favorite with the male cats, especially Grayfur. Actually, she gets along well with most of the cats.

SARAH PRINCESS HARTMAN ROOS
ALPHARETTA, GEORGIA

Sarah is a beautiful white calico kitty. She knows her name well and prefers Sarah over Kitty Kitty. She is a lover of curtains. When she wants to stretch out by climbing the drapes, she looks as if she's doing pull-ups. We love her very much. Her birthdate is August 1989.

SASHA ADELMAN
WINFIELD, ILLINOIS

Sasha, a senior citizen feline, was the smallest of her litter when adopted at four months of age. Her generosity allows humans to share her home as long as her living requirements are met. She demands ice cubes in her water cup, the litter pan cleaned after each use, a cushioned chair next to a particular window as the optimal sunning spot, and a lap to snuggle in when desired. It is our pleasure to meet her every wish. We love her. Sasha adored her brother Kodiak, with whom she lived and played for over twenty years, and mourns his death.

SCARFACE CARTER
LEXINGTON, NORTH CAROLINA

Scarface: wild, stray, bony, wart on nose, bad eye, crumpled ear. He started hanging around our house, and after a little love is tame, fat, good eye, straight ear, but still wart on nose. Testing his nine lives, Scarface got caught in a truck fan belt and spent one and a half months in the hospital. Even with all the hardships, he's turned out to be one tough cat! We adopted Scarface, and in return he gives us gentle love and on occasion a rat or two.

SCARLI ESKALYO
BAY SHORE, NEW YORK

Scarli, a year and a half old, is a Persian/British Shorthair mix. He will race you to the sink, as he loves to drink from the faucet if you turn it on. His way of greeting you in the morning is to collapse to the floor and roll over on his back. His favorite sleeping spot is between the pillows on the bed, and he likes to sit on top of the washing machine when there's someone in the laundry room. If you're sitting at the kitchen table eating, he will tap you with his paw until you give him a snack.

SCHATTEN KITTY SILVER
NORTH CANTON, OHIO

Born in New Jersey, Schatten is twenty years old, black and white, shorthaired, and looks like Socks the First Kitty. She is a snob who prefers only me but would rather be left alone completely. Schatten loves to eat mushrooms and pepperoni and drink Snapple. At her age, she doesn't do much anymore and I give her her way all the time because she's earned it—even if it means wanting to eat at two in the morning. I hope she lives twenty more years!

SCHATZY BATES
COLORADO SPRINGS, COLORADO

Beautiful Schatzy is tan, orange, and black, a pure tortoise cat. The name Schatzy is German for "dearie" or "darling," and she certainly is that. She's ten pounds plus, with short, thick hair, and will be nine years old in October. Schatzy is very playful and has always been a one-person cat. She shares her home currently on a sailboat with Hershey and is at home anyplace as long as her mistress is there. Her favorite toy of many years is a pink fuzzy duck that squeaks when she tosses it about. She does this when she wants to play or get attention.

SCHMOO ("MOOBEY") CLARKE
DALLAS, TEXAS

Schmoo is a solid-black two-year-old. She has just recently started to go outside and loves it. She crouches down low to the ground and pounces on anything that moves. She never kills anything, just plays with it. Schmoo sleeps with us every night, usually under the sheets and comforter next to our feet. She's a big help around the house, keeping her brother Hamlet (a pig) clean by licking him. Schmoo is such a sweet and gentle kitty—we're very lucky to have her in the family.

SCORPIO ("MAMA'S BIG BOY") YOERGER
LAS VEGAS, NEVADA

Scorpio is a gray tiger-striped cat with a bold white chest and number one of the four cats I now have. Being the oldest (ten years) and the only male, he acts as leader of the pack. When he calls, the girls come running. He's an instigator of fun and trouble, announcing that it's playtime. He loves to be petted by just about anyone, going from one person to the next in a room full of people. But he always saves his special hugs for Mom.

SEBASTEON ALDAZ SYVERSON
WICHITA, KANSAS

Nine-year-old Sebasteon is white with one green eye and one blue eye. He is polydactyl, with six toes on each paw. An international traveler, he has gone from Florida to Athens, Greece, to Kansas. Even though he enjoys human companionship, Sebasteon strongly dislikes being held. His favorite sleeping places include a beanbag chair and the electric blanket. Always an early riser, Sebasteon is a dependable alarm clock but with no snooze button. His loud meow and penetrating stare promptly announce it's breakfast time. Of course, eating is Sebasteon's favorite pastime.

SHADDOW ROUNDS
SCOTTSBLUFF, NEBRASKA

My cat Shaddow is one year old. He is black, white, and gray with green eyes. He was in a litter of six. Shaddow weighs eight pounds. He is an ornery cat, but he is a sweet cat, too. He is different from most cats since he chases dogs instead of letting the dogs chase him. If Shaddow is missing, we know where to find him: either sleeping in the washer or dryer, or hiding in the plants. If he's outside, he's usually in the flowers. When he wants attention, Shaddow bites us gently until we pet him.

SHADOW ("BEAR") VON MERTENS
CULVER CITY, CALIFORNIA

S hadow was born on June 5, 1987. He was the only male in a litter of six kittens. He is a little overweight and doesn't really like to move much. Sometimes I think he's too lazy to meow—he just opens his mouth and nothing comes out. His favorite non-activities are eating and lying on his back in the path of travel. The only exercise he gets is running from our older female cat, Whisper, who weighs about one-half as much. But setting aside his timid, temperamental, intolerant personality, we will always love him like a child.

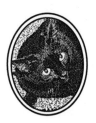

SHADOW LAMONT (CRANSTON) MILLER
AMERICAN FORK, UTAH

S hadow is a silver tabby adopted as an adult stray. He loves owning a person but is still adjusting to the world of humans and three other cats. He vocalizes a lot and earned his name, "The Shadow," initially because he was frequently heard but not seen. He loves to play with his food and catches crunchies in midair with his paws. Although he tries to be macho, Shadow is a cream puff at heart—and belly. Weighing seventeen pounds, he seems to live by the philosophy "It is, therefore I eat it." Even orange juice!

SHADY HAUGEN
TOLEDO, OHIO

Shady, a Seal Point Himalayan cat, is a very lovable guy who likes people. He likes to wake you up in the morning. His gentle technique is purring and putting his whiskers in your face. When he is hungry, he kneads the back of your leg to get your attention. He does quite well in opening vanity and closet doors. His favorite toys are plastic rings and a twirling leather shoelace. His hiding place is the seat of a chair under the table. He and his brother, Sunny, have a cat nanny named Elaine.

SHATZIE MUSSELMAN
TWELVE MILE, INDIANA

She's a black-and-white Bobtail shorthair. She likes to press her mouth against my cheek. She also likes to put her paws under my neck and knead; in fact, she keeps me awake at night sometimes doing it. Shatzie enjoys playing ball. She'll run all over the house, batting and carrying a ball around. She once stole a hard-boiled egg off the table and ran around with it in her mouth. I can only assume she thought it was a ball. Except to her surprise, she could eat it! I love her very much.

SHARDA PHEA HANSHAW
YARDLEY, PENNSYLVANIA

Sharda is a nine-year-old Seal Point Himalayan, but don't tell her—she has no idea. She's a dainty, blue-eyed, spoiled purrer who loves to cuddle. Wherever you are, Sharda is. She listens and will come, follow, sit, or lie, as you ask her. A constant talker, she lets you know what she wants, or how badly, by her meows. Her most demanding calls are to be brushed. Sharda loves flowers, watching her TV video, wearing sweaters, but most of all her son, Zackery. Her greatest asset is making you feel special—she definitely has charm.

SHEBA ALEKSIC
ESCONDIDO, CALIFORNIA

O ur beautiful best friend is a kitty. She looks like a purebred ragdoll, but she's our little mutt. She has charmed everyone she's met since being selected from a box at a garage sale eight years ago. So much money has been spent on toys, but her favorite has always been a simple piece of ribbon. Sheba is one of the most fortunate animals in the world. She watches from inside her home the many strays her owners care for and knows she is the lucky one, since she doesn't have to go outside and face the cruel world.

SILVER BABY MUSSELMAN
TWELVE MILE, INDIANA

Silver Baby is a tabby with silver and black stripes. She is the orneriest cat we've ever had. Her favorite sport is seeing how much she can bug me when I'm cooking. You'd think she's a starving cat the way she begs for food! She's always on the lookout for a fly. If she sees one, she'll tear the house apart trying to get to it. You have to get to it as soon as possible to save the house. But she's a sweetie and we love her.

SIME MUSSELMAN
TWELVE MILE, INDIANA

Sime is part Siamese with beautiful blue eyes. She's very affectionate and loves to rub her feet on your leg. (Thank goodness, she's declawed.) She's the only cat I've ever seen that always has her tail straight up in the air. Her nickname is "Flag Pole" because of that. She won't let you hold her, and she won't lie with you, but she's constantly walking on *you* when you lie down. She's a sweetie and loved very much.

SIR LANCELOT REIMANN
FEDERAL WAY, WASHINGTON

Sir Lancelot is quite a celebrity, having been in *Who's Who of Animals, I Love Cats, The Everett Herald, The Wall Street Journal, Uncommon Cats*, ACFA's *Parade of Royalty, Cat Chat, Kitty Kat Courier,* and *Pet Pals*, and having had a poem published about him in *Allusions*. People come and go in our lives, but the kitty always remains with his unconditional love and acceptance, to see you through the good and bad times that life may throw your way. Lancelot and his big gold eyes are such an integral part of my life that I'd be lost without him.

SIR WINSTON GRAHAM
ATLANTA, GEORGIA

Quiet and unassuming, Sir Winston has been there during many times of life changes. From a small black coal ball, he has grown into a shy but loving cat who knows when to comfort. His favorite way of showing affection is to lie on my pillow or take up too much space on my bed or chair. His favorite pastime is perching on the windowsill for hours and watching the birds fly by. He is insightful and knows when I need a friend. However, when I travel, he lets me know of his dissatisfaction by lying on my travel bag and hiding my jewelry!

SISSY CAT PORTZ
FAYETTEVILLE, NORTH CAROLINA

Sissy Cat is a Manx with no tail at all and long rear legs that enable her to jump very high. She is several shades of brown and gold with a white mane. She is shy but likes to be groomed. She eats Korean food and especially enjoys a good spinach salad. She often touches her water with her paw before getting a drink from the far side of the bowl. Her favorite thing in the whole world is her brother Rover; she keeps him groomed and always goes to his rescue when he gets into trouble.

SKEETER MUSSELMAN
TWELVE MILE, INDIANA

Skeeter is a yellow-and-white-striped short-hair with legs as long as a giraffe's. He'll wrap those legs around your neck and give you hugs. He's definitely a lap cat. He loves to eat peanuts—you can very quietly open the can and he'll still hear it and come running. He was only a couple of weeks old when we got him and raised him on a bottle. He was as little as a mosquito, so we named him Skeeter. He's one of our favorite cats, and we love him dearly.

SLUGGER ("BUGGY") PASCOE
TRAVERSE CITY, MICHIGAN

He's an apricot-and-white, ten-pound, long-haired handsome fellow. With eight toes on each foot, he jumps, lands, and balances himself with the greatest of ease. A sportsman, a protector of home and family, he fearlessly patrols his territory and manages it all—without any claws! He puts the puppy in his place with utter authority and is a better alarm clock than any we've ever had (if only he could let us sleep in past 5 A.M. on weekends).

SMOKEY ROYER
WHITEHALL, PENNSYLVANIA

Smokey is a gray shorthair with beautiful green eyes and a light gray patch on his nose that makes him so cute. He was found wandering the streets by a nice policeman who brought him to the shelter and that's when I adopted him. Smokey is a real sweetie-pie. He's affectionate and playful. His favorite things to play with are sponge balls, feather dusters, and bread clips. When I come home, he's always there to greet me and give me a great big Eskimo kiss. And whenever he's in my room he'll cuddle up next to me and sleep.

SMOKIE
HUNTINGTON BEACH, CALIFORNIA

Smokie was born April 13, 1985. He is probably the smartest cat I have ever known. Smokie is a large cat, standing about fourteen inches (at the shoulder) and weighing in at fourteen pounds. He is a beautiful smoky gray color and will lie around the house like an Egyptian Sphinx. More like a dog than a cat, Smokie performs tricks on command. He is the hit of the evenings as he gives the best massage there is! Just lie on your stomach and he'll be there with those huge paws; he'll move up or down, just tell him!

SMUDGE NEWMAN
GRAY, TENNESSEE

Smudge is sleek, white, fluffy, and gorgeous! Her loving, affectionate nature endears her to all but unfortunately makes her an easy mark for neighborhood troublemakers! Her collection of battle wounds is impressive and she wears them proudly, albeit reluctantly. Her favorite hobby is championship wrestling on the kitchen floor with her brother, Bijou, and perfecting her manicure on your flesh. She is a true jewel.

SNOWBALL KAMEN
WINDSOR, ONTARIO, CANADA

She was my first love. White as snow. Not a blemish on her. I called her Snowball. She was the first thing I held close to my heart and loved. When I sat down, she came and sat beside me, her tush pushing into my side. And when I lay down, she lay beside me. She licked my hand as if there were no end. She sat in my lap for comfort. The only thing that ever loved unselfishly. My cat.

SNOWBALL SEABURY
MORRIS, ALABAMA

Snowball is a white cat. Born in 1978, she survived surgery at five weeks of age to remove a cattle grub from her neck—and has been a survivor ever since. Her favorite game is rattling a doorknob at night and running when you get up to let her in. This game can entertain her several times in a single night. She enjoys snacking on popcorn or corn on the cob and squeezing herself into any box within her reach. She does not bathe herself but has spent many years licking on her Poodle friend, Tina, trying to get the kinks out of her hair.

SNUGGLES BUSH
WESTMINSTER, MARYLAND

Snuggles is my cat, a Blue Point Himalayan. He has beautiful blue eyes and a big bushy tail. He acts more like a dog than a cat. He sits up like a dog when he wants attention and follows my every activity in the house. He loves to play hide-and-seek and tears around rooms and up and down our steps, sliding on the rugs and meowing with glee. He is strictly a house cat, and his playful actions instill a happy attitude in my own personality. Snuggles even enjoys sleeping all night beside me on my pillow.

SOPHIE KRENEK
IRVINE, CALIFORNIA

An abandoned cat left in the cold . . .
That's how we got Sophie.
The story's old.
A sweeter cat you couldn't ask for,
She walked into our hearts through the back
   door.
Hurt, scared, and sick, with a few aches and pains,
But, lucky us, we never heard any complaints.
She has but two teeth, but boy, can she eat!
As an indoor cat, declawing gave her sore feet.
A tumor took her eye, but she never put up
   a stink—
As a matter of fact, she now gives us that
   knowing wink.
We're fortunate to have a cat like Sophie,
No teeth, no claws, one eye, but ours . . . totally!

SOX CONWAY
NEWTOWN, CONNECTICUT

Born in New Rochelle, New York, Sox has the distinction of being part Manx. This has left her with only a partial tail and large hindquarters. Her long white whiskers stand out against her black velvet fur. Named for her white-dipped toes, Sox also has a white bib on her chest and a bikini bottom. Sox, the Queen, will talk when asked to speak and becomes very concerned when her mom is in the shower. In her youth Sox perfected the "Amazing Kitty Flip" and continues to love to play and go for walks outside.

SPECIAL LIEBERMAN
ROSLYN HEIGHTS, NEW YORK

Special, our cream-and-gray tabby, is the most loving cat in the world. The runt of his litter, he is now a strong seventeen pounds at age twelve. Special loves walking around the neighborhood with his owners. No leash, he just walks along. A very vocal cat, he can let you know exactly what he wants, from having his litter box changed to a treat out of the refrigerator. His favorite place to sleep is in bed with the comforter pulled up over his head. His favorite activity is playing with a Q-Tip in a running stream of water at the sink!

SPOOK CORK-SAMPLES (A.K.A. SPOOKI, BAT FACE)
CLINTON TOWNSHIP, MICHIGAN

Spook is all black with short hair and a gentle manner until the devil gets in his emerald green eyes—then watch out! Another thing peculiar to Spook is that his fangs are abnormally long, giving him a vampire look. His favorite position is on his back. I would suppose he thinks the world cockeyed and this straightens it out. He also loves to do sit-ups and exercise with us. He is much like Mr. Mistafolies (*Cats*) in that he isn't where he is and is where he isn't. Alas, however, this brave devil cat is deathly afraid of the out-of-doors!

SPOOK KESSINGER
BOISE, IDAHO

S pook was born on a farm, the son of a tabby mother and a wild bobcat father. He looked like his striped mother, but in the sun his orange-yellow undercoat showed through. His hind legs were taller than most, and his short tail stuck straight up in the air about five inches. Spook was a most loving and intelligent cat. My bedroom light dimmer switch was just out of my reach from the bed, and Spook delighted in getting on the headboard and turning the light on bright repeatedly. Once I took one of my "harem" slippers away from him, only to find that he had a mouse in it!

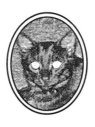

SPOOK NEELD
SOMERS POINT, NEW JERSEY

Born in 1985, on Halloween, Spook is a very small, very cute black cat. He doesn't have a tail, so you can always admire his sexy walk. Spook enjoys sparring with his sister, Ninja the Dog, and usually wins. He also likes hiding in boxes and drawers. When he's ready to play, he'll roll over on his back and let you rub his furry belly. In his spare time, he loves sleeping and throwing up.

SPOOKY COCHRAN
CARMEN, IDAHO

Spooky, a coal-black cat with "glow in the dark" eyes, was lucky to be found by a special lady who loves animals and always has room for one more at her ranch. Spooky lives with friends Marvin and Atila and several other cats as well as dogs, horses, and cows. Each morning, after eating his Cheerios, he loyally goes with the lady rancher and does the chores. It's never too hot or too cold—Spooky always goes! After a full day of ranching, Spooky looks forward to his favorite treat: ice cream.

SPROCKET SAPP
WINSTON SALEM, NORTH CAROLINA

Sprocket was so tiny and gray. After surviving a cold winter storm, my friend Kathy found him hidden in a car engine. He was a "fraidy" cat. I thought he might grow up under the dresser, where he stayed all the time. At night, he would sneak on my pillow and sleep for a while. Now, when the lights go off at night, he sleeps on his own pillow right next to me. He might be spoiled, as he eats a lot of tuna and salmon. But he depends on me and that makes him very special!

SPY FLECK
FAYETTEVILLE, NORTH CAROLINA

Spy is a marmalade shorthair tabby, also known as the Kissing Cat. He loves to kiss. After a request for a kiss, he'll press his nose on the recipient's lips. Female visitors don't have to ask! Spy has a bath ritual that he likes to perform. He waits while I shower in a safe dry towel area. When the water stops, he begins calling until I'm safely out of the shower, wrapped in towels. At this time he reaches up to be held and wrapped in a towel. He then proceeds to croodle and act out in kitten-type behaviors. This is our quality time.

STANLEY ("KING AZUL") GIUNTOLI
SEYMOUR, CONNECTICUT

One word describes Stanley: irresistible. This beautiful cream-colored cat, with black and gray tiger markings, has bright green eyes. He knows he's gorgeous and uses his looks to get whatever he wants, which is food. His constant mission, from the moment he awakes, is to find food. Don't try eating without sharing with Stanley. He'll cry like he hasn't eaten in years—a definite Academy Award-winning feline. If he wraps around your shoulders, it's because he wants to grab at your spoon with his paw! My husband and I love Stanley with all our hearts.

STORMY AND PERI
SOUTHPORT, CONNECTICUT

One day a car pulled up in Stormy's driveway. We introduced Peri to Stormy. They said hello and instantly liked each other. They're best friends now, and they sleep on the same blanket, play together, and fight with each other. Stormy steps on Peri's neck, and Peri bites Stormy. Then they make up and go roll in some nice cool mud. Stormy is big, Peri is small. Stormy is black, Peri is white. Stormy is male, Peri is female. Stormy grins, Peri scowls. Stormy is Jewish, Peri is Buddhist. Stormy loves Peri, Peri loves Stormy.

STUSSY
FAIRBANKS, ALASKA

Stussy is my seventeen-pound yellow tomcat. He is a very fickle cat. Sometimes he walks around knocking stuff off the tables and counters. He likes to come into my room at night and lick my eyelids when he wants love. In the mornings, he comes into the bathrooms and helps us floss our teeth by pulling on the floss. When he's hungry, he knocks his food dish off the washer at someone who walks by. In the summer time, Stussy brings home animals that he's killed, like birds and shrews, and leaves them on the porch. Stussy is my most favorite pet.

SUNNY HAUGEN
TOLEDO, OHIO

Sunny is a Cream Point Himalayan cat who likes to greet you when you come home. He is protective, a leader, and likes attention. He knows when to meow, say "now" to get his own way, or say "ow" when getting brushed. He likes to catch his own shadows and play inside brown paper bags. He will give cat kisses if he feels like it. His favorite toy is a round red circle with seeded eyes on it. He likes to lie down and have his belly scratched, too! He has a brother named Shady. It's a pleasure to have an adorable cat like Sunny.

SUZYUKI GELLER
BRANDON, FLORIDA

Suzyuki is a Seal Point Snowshoe—a pretty breed of cat with dark brown face and legs and white "snowshoe" paws. She is an active acrobat and also a retriever! She loves to chase a homemade catnip-filled calico heart, bring it back, drop it on your shoes, and meow for you to toss it again. Suzyuki makes a game of eating: she flips each piece of dry food out of her bowl and chases it, then nibbles. She's great fun to watch . . . and play with . . . and try to figure out!

436

SWEETIE PIE HALL
DURHAM, NORTH CAROLINA

Sweetie is a longhaired, all-white cat with olive-colored eyes and rose-pink ears and nose. She traces her ancestry to Nefertiti and Cleopatra and carries herself accordingly. As she walks in dignified grace, she communicates with her tail, always held high. When inspection of her domain is completed, she retreats to her favorite chair; there, she bathes herself and then uses her tail like a fan to cover all but her eyes and ears. Sweetie's gift to her loved ones is choosing one of their laps instead of her favorite chair.

SWEETUMS
BOULDER, COLORADO

Sweetums is the keeper of my heart! A gray, eight-pound fluff-ball of fur, whose purring constantly reminds me of the love she holds in her little kitty heart! Each night Sweetums insists upon snuggling with me and comes under the covers to nestle softly against my heart. Her love is unconditional. She does not care how I look, how much money I have, or how out-of-date my clothes might be. She adds a tenderness and caring to my life more than any human has ever managed to do. Only a true cat lover can fully comprehend this sort of feline love!

SWIX COOPER
GLENS FALLS, NEW YORK

Swix is an alley cat with a very laid-back attitude. He is white with black spots like a cow, which is why we call him our Moo Kitty. Swix likes to feel as if he owns the house—and most of the time he does. In the summer, he loves to sleep sprawled out in open windows. In the winter, he's usually found in the living room recliner. No matter what you feed him, he'll eat it, although his favorite food is cantaloupe. The most unique thing about Swix is his name, which comes from a ski wax.

SYLVESTER GREEN
STATEN ISLAND, NEW YORK

Sylvester is a black-and-white cat who greatly appreciates being rescued from the street in 1988. Occasional gifts—mice, birds, and butterflies—are left for his owners, a.k.a. Mom and Dad! He follows them around the house and yard, overseeing their every move. An owner's shoulders, arms or lap are fair game for him to cuddle in. Just like a baby, he insists on being picked up. He has his own fishing pole to play with and drinks out of the bird's bath. He vacations in Vermont but doesn't care for the four-hour car ride to get there.

TABBY TIP KIRCHBERG
LAKEWOOD, COLORADO

Tabby hails from a farm just south of the city. Moving to the city was indeed quite an adjustment for her, but her human, Joanne, gave her plenty of time. She now has her own room, in which stands a solitary chair that serves as her throne. Whether sleeping on her throne or curled next to the heating vent, she resembles a black bowling ball with brown and white spots. Her only other habit is a constant nervous twitch in her tail.

TABITHA COOPER
GLENS FALLS, NEW YORK

At the age of one and a half years, this bug-catching feline cannot sit still. She never wants to be held but waits by the door to be let outside. Tabitha is a calico cat with four white paws and a white patch under her neck. It's easy to tell she's a girl by the way she sits and because of her constant meowing. She also always goes where she isn't supposed to. Watching the coffee perk in the morning and walking all around the kitchen counters are some of her more popular sports.

TABITHA GABRIELLE ("TABBY GABBY") GODFREY
CANTON, OHIO

Tabby is a black-and-white domestic cat. She was a gift from my husband, who got her for me when she was eight weeks old from the Humane Society. Tabby was our first pet, and all she did was eat and sleep and zoom all over the house like a dart of lightning. Now, when I have the typewriter on the floor, she loves to type. She is a contortionist kitty—her arms, legs, and belly go every which way when she sleeps. I let her sleep with me at night, but when she wakes me up at 4 A.M. to eat, that's when she gets thrown out of bed!

TAFFY
LIGHTHOUSE POINT, FLORIDA

Taffy is a sixteen-pound calico who looks like she's black and white from one side and brown and white from the other. She wakes her owners up daily by butting heads and then waits in the bathroom to be combed with a wet comb. After her bathroom grooming, she (nags) meows nonstop until she's fed. Then she goes off to find a place to clean herself and sleep the day away till her owners return from work. She is very affectionate and has to be touching whoever she decides to sit next to or on.

TANK
SALT LAKE CITY, UTAH

Tank is our three-year-old feline son. He has short jet-black fur and big beautiful yellow eyes, and he's always in the mood to be loved. He spends his days romping across the sofas and endlessly dreaming of fields of catnip. When the opportunity arises, he sneaks out the door to bathe in the brightest star or become one with the flower bed. Strutting back in the house, he's the color of dirt and feels like he's on top of the world. He's always a gentleman, and life would never be the same without him.

TAR WINDSCHITL
WEST MELBOURNE, FLORIDA

Tar was born on our bathroom floor in the early morning of May 18, 1980. His small, tricolored mother (Mocha) gave him his black coat with a white "diaper," and he has the largeness and longer hair of his father (a Main Coon). He's aloof, but when he wants attention, he really demands it—usually by planting himself at face level right on top of the newspaper you're reading. He knows where the catnip is kept and has trained his human grandmother to give him some, using the loud vocal commands he uses to get your attention.

TARA LYSAUGHT
KANSAS CITY, KANSAS

Tara is a tortoiseshell cat, mostly black with cream and orange. She is nicknamed "the Enforcer" because she comes running anytime I raise my voice to any of the other pets. She has the loudest purr I have ever heard, and I have had many cats through the years. She is muscular, but can stand on top of a closet door and turn around with no effort. Though she has no front claws, she is an efficient mouser and, unfortunately, on occasion a bird catcher. At age ten, Tara still acts like a kitten.

TASHA RUSSO
SOUTH GATE, CALIFORNIA

Tasha is a ten-year-old black-and-gray Persian and Angora cat. She's very spoiled. I call her my juvenile delinquent on four legs. She has some strange habits. She sits on her toys or rocks or anything small. Just like a chicken. She also baas just like a sheep when I tell her no. And sometimes, when she gets silly or excited, she stands on her back paws and hops across the room. Just like a rabbit.

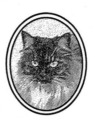

TATER TAT CAIRNS
MOOERS, NEW YORK

I found her in a loft when she was about ten days old and fed her four times a day with an eyedropper for the first three weeks. She does not meow like any other cat, but she peeps. She must taste of whatever I am eating: veggies, asparagus, lettuce, broccoli, and potatoes (from which she gets her name). She keeps the house free from flies and mosquitoes, and in doing so she is destroying the drapes and curtains. When she sees a fly, she bats it with her paw and does not miss. She never goes outside and is always at the door to greet me and get a pat.

TC THOMAS
COCOA BEACH, FLORIDA

This fluffy gray cat has an untamed, king-of-the-jungle arrogance. He was semi-wild, but adopted "his dog" Sandpiper and eventually adopted the people, too. He's a cat pretending to be a dog: faithful, full of love and full of his own spirit. For a time, he herded small Florida lizards—keeping dozens in the house, corraled under dining room chairs and trapped in window miniblinds. Tossing live lizards in the bed at 4 A.M. was a favorite amusement. Now he surveys his beach, monitors his pelicans, plays godfather to his kitten neighbors—and still delights in 4 A.M. play.

TEDDY JUDGE
GOOSE LAKE, IOWA

Teddy is a black cat with big yellow eyes and a tail that is two inches long. We all believe he's really a human in "cat's fur" by the way he loves people food, sleeps on the spare bedroom water bed, and talks to us. His favorite game is hide-and-seek, but he doesn't always play by the rules. His favorite food is tuna, with black olives running a close second. He also requires us to pet him the whole time that he's eating. Teddy is definitely a very, very spoiled cat!

THACKERAY
CHICAGO, ILLINOIS

Thackeray is a seventeen-year-old tabby born in the shadow of statesman Henry Clay's home in Lexington, Kentucky. After spending his first year on the University of Kentucky campus, this Kentucky Wildcat set off for Chicago, his current home. The big city made Thackeray aware of the culinary treats available to the aggressive feline. He ranks pepperoni, Yankee pot roast, and gyros among his favorite treats. A connoisseur of fine catnip, he frequently samples the savory blends grown in his backyard. Thackeray spends his retirement years stealing from the kitchen table and marking his territory.

THE BRUCE AHLBERG
NASHVILLE, TENNESSEE

B ruce was tiny enough to fit in the palm of my hand when he joined the family. His allergy to milk may force him to eat special food, but it hasn't stopped him from growing to the size of a normal eight-year-old. Bruce likes to spend quality time with his fish friend, Guido, and help him drink the water in his fishbowl. A Texan by birth, he enjoys playing with plastic toy guns and sunbathing on his perch.

THE MISSY AHLBERG
SPRINGFIELD, ILLINOIS

Missy was discovered as a crying lump by the side of the road. Being a Manx, she earned her name because she is "missing" her tail. Known affectionately as FDR, Missy loves to sit in her basket or on her perch and survey her domain. Her difficult burdens in life include the dreaded vacuum cleaner, having to eat diet pellets (supplemented by milk from the bottom of the cereal bowl), enduring new family members, and dealing with people who keep moving her litter box.

THOMAS BABINGTON MACAULAY FOULKE
LEWISTOWN, PENNSYLVANIA

Macaulay roamed around the neighborhood, starving, friendless, and alone, for several years before he decided he could trust me. Now Macaulay is a gorgeous pumpkin-colored tabby. He still goes outside, but he stays close to the home he loves. For quite a while, he was kept apart from my other cats since two were not well and I wished to avoid undue stress. Anything was okay with Macaulay. He was grateful for his comfy bed and regular meals. Now he is a real part of the family, a sweet guy.

THOMASINA FOULKE
LEWISTOWN, PENNSYLVANIA

Thomasina is "charcoal" blue. For several months she arrived every afternoon on my front steps. She was too frightened to eat the food I put out until I was gone. She was very thin, full of anxiety. After a while she decided I was one of the good guys, so she moved in. Now she carries herself proudly and purrs me awake every morning. She even gets a mite testy if her meals are not quite ready when *she* is ready to eat.

THUNDER MIGHT ("GRANDMA") HUNTER
MARINETTE, WISCONSIN

Thunder is an Angora cat with tiger stripes on her face and tail. She mostly sleeps now, since she is eighteen years old. She has touched the lives of many people who are no longer with us. In her younger days she was very active. I will never forget the day she caught her first bumblebee. It was huge. It took both her paws to cover it and in her mouth it went. It was amazing—she never got stung. Thunder wandered into our family's life as a stray, and she has a heart of gold with an extraordinary spirit.

TIBBIE PARKER
RIVER HEIGHTS, UTAH

Tibbie (better known as Roonie) is a pure-bred Siamese. He only likes certain people, and he wants them to make a *big* fuss over him. He uses the house for a race track to see how fast he can get from one end to the other. He sleeps during the day in a wash basin. At night he sleeps with our son, since he feels he is his guardian and protector. He meows at a vigorous rate until he is recognized and fed in the mornings (starts about 5 A.M.). But Tibbie (Roonie) is the most lovable fifteen-pound cat you could find on earth!

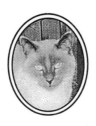

458

TIFFY WORKMAN
MADISON, TENNESSEE

Tiffy is the Siamese cat who rules our home. Although she has us trained pretty much to her liking, she still finds it necessary to supervise almost everything we do. She especially enjoys helping us make beds and rake leaves. Her favorite foods are chicken, ice cream, and any kind of cheese. She is terrified of thunder and noisy children. She hides until the danger has passed. She enjoys playing with little fur mice and playing chase with her brothers, Poo Poo and Pretty Boy. She is very mischievous but also very sweet and loving.

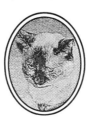

459

TIGA PENA
SUNNYVALE, CALIFORNIA

Tiga is a tabby cat. He is Maria's cat—she found him outside as a stray baby kitten. He is funny and likes to chase after Patches, our other cat. Tiga is one year old and jumps like a kangaroo. He often sits in the bathroom while you take a shower or hides in an empty box. When you talk to him, he answers you back. He enjoys going out in the car to parks or festivals. Tiga is nosy and plays the little investigator, especially if the adults are eating. Tiga is very much loved.

TIGER MCGRIFF
MONTCLAIR, NEW JERSEY

Tiger is a striped cat weighing fifteen pounds. He is completely blind. For a long time we didn't know he was blind because he gets around quite well. Tiger is a happy cat. He likes to put his face in Father's shoes or sneakers when he takes them off and go to sleep.

461

TIGGER BROECKER-HALL
VIRGINIA BEACH, VIRGINIA

Tigger is everything that the name implies. She is a light silver tabby, weighs eight pounds and can vertically jump about four and a half feet, especially when trying to catch a fly. Besides fly-catching, her only mission in life is to play with string—until her sister hides it. Tigger wags her tail more than most dogs do. She is always ready to play and must be in the middle of everything. For a cat, she is man's best friend.

TIGGER ("GRAY THING") HANDSCHUH
WHITE PLAINS, NEW YORK

This two-year-old gray tabby speaks her mind. Found abandoned as a kitten alongside the road, she gives her thanks tenfold every time she washes the fingers of her mistress or kneads her claws gently on her mistress's winter sweaters. Tigger is an expert hunter and tree climber, but she enjoys snoozing in bed when day is done. She is a loyal spirit who braves water to accompany her mistress to the bathroom. She loves people and things that crawl, hop, or slither. She is long of whisker and mischievous to a fault.

TIGGER RANEY
COCOA, FLORIDA

Tigger is what I call a throwback in the genes. He was born from a calico and a stray tomcat and is one of the most beautiful cats I've seen. He is a longhaired tiger stripe, and his markings are astounding and emphasize his bright green eyes. He likes to spend time out in the grass, on his leash. I started him on a leash when he was six weeks old so he wouldn't stray. He doesn't mind his leash, and when I open the door he'll go to the end of the porch and wait for me to put it on.

TIKI MATHEWS
FEDERAL WAY, WASHINGTON

Tiki is a blue-eyed Siamese-mix kitty. I say kitty because at age two he's never grown up. The word "yang" meowed out and running and hiding will start the game. He comes and finds us and then runs so we'll chase him. Meowing loudly, he'll crouch down or flop on his side for some gentle roughing up. Then we run and hide again and he chases us. He also breaks into the closet to get his string toy and drag it out and around the house until someone picks it up and plays with him.

TINA MARIE WELLS
PHILADELPHIA, PENNSYLVANIA

Tina Marie was a tiny little thing that appeared at my back door in the summer of 1989. She is such a pretty little girl, my Tina Marie. Petite and sweet, she has never scratched or shown any kind of aggressive behavior. Tina Marie sits in front of my plate at mealtime and guards it while I eat. Of course, she's there to lap up any stray crumbs. And if I should blink an eye, mysteriously there's food missing from my plate and, for good reason, Tina Marie is licking her lips. Tina Marie looks like her name. A real sweetheart. Born in June of 1989.

TINGA TRULL
IRVING, TEXAS

Tinga is a black tortoiseshell cat. She is very affectionate and loves to be kissed on her forehead. She also loves to be brushed and rocked to sleep. Her favorite toy is a big brown paper sack. Her favorite treats are sliced turkey from the deli and chocolate Häagen-Dazs ice cream. Her favorite place to sleep is on my shoulder with her head tucked under my chin. When she's really trying to get my attention, she'll talk to me—she can say "Mama"! (For all nonbelievers, I have her tape-recorded!)

TINKERBELL KUBELDIS
HUNTINGTON BEACH, CALIFORNIA

Born in May, 1980, Tinker is the oldest of five cats. She loves playing with lizards, even after getting a piece of her tongue bitten off. Her best friend was Maggie, a Golden Retriever; they were inseparable, and Tink would climb up on top of the refrigerator and steal dog treats for her. Tink never liked typical people games like petting or TLC and would swat anyone who tried. After losing her best buddy Mag, she became sick and nearly died. Now, since recovering, a new personality has emerged—sort of a composite of Tink and Mag.

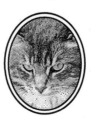

TOBY JOHNS BELLISARIO
PITTSBURGH, PENNSYLVANIA

Toby is a coal-black shorthair who prides himself on the lush, high-gloss coat and amber eyes that landed him a nonspeaking role in the film *Two Evil Eyes*, based on Edgar Allan Poe's *The Black Cat*. He also had the pleasure of perching himself atop the Stanley Cup and having been featured in a newspaper article. Stardom has not affected him, though. A true Renaissance cat, Toby is at home sitting in the bay window, gazing outside while listening to his favorite opera arias; stalking wildlife; curling upon a comfortable lap; and, of course, catnapping.

TOM STATON
MADISON HEIGHTS, VIRGINIA

Tom is a solid-gray Norwegian Forest Cat who loves to hunt. He likes to be near us and follow us around. He refuses to come when we call him and even pretends not to hear us. He likes to be rubbed, but will not tolerate being picked up or held. He doesn't like to be brushed, either. Knocking on the door with his paws and waiting to be fed is his favorite activity. He runs the house, but we love him.

TOM CAT KILBORN
DENVER, COLORADO

L ooking through Tom Cat's eyes, a lot has changed in this world. Discovered roaming the alleys of Capitol Hill in the summer of 1980, he soon became legendary for his incredible ability to assist the continuation of his species. It took over a year's time, but he was soon coaxed into a life of ease and warmth. Once a wild animal, he now enjoys being petted and sleeping with his human, Scott. Confirmed known descendants: Phootsie Kirchberg. Unconfirmed known descendants: too numerous to mention.

TOMKEY C. MOORE
FAIRBANKS, ALASKA

A classic black longhaired cat with green eyes, like those painted by Sue Boetcher and other artists, Tomkey loves the Alaskan out-of-doors. When his mistress is snow-shoeing, he follows. In snow-covered spring, he sniffs at bare spots of earth, imagining summer. He loves to smell flowers and insists on order. Like a black Sphinx, he represents true repose as he guards his home. Although he's not a lap cat, he yields to his mother's whims, even to wearing a red hat to amuse summer visitors (though he probably laughs the hardest!). Once abandoned, this ten-year-old cat is the delight of his human mommy.

TOMMY ("SMOKEY") DUMPSTER
SALIDA, COLORADO

Smokey isn't your typical cat. He was abandoned in a trash dumpster and found by our friend, Matthew Barela, who called to ask if I would take him. I said, "Yes, he will be a wonderful surprise for Rosa, my daughter." Matthew drove 460 miles round-trip bringing Smokey to his new home. Smokey will be two years old. He has filled our lives with many entertaining moments. He plays Fetch with rubber bands and small paper toys. When he's finished playing, he'll take his rubber band or toy and drop it in his dry food dish. He's a comical kitty.

TOPAZ BURLEY (A.K.A. GROPAZ)
ELKRIDGE, MARYLAND

Topaz is a twenty-three-pound shorthaired redhead tabby. He was a present in July of 1987. He really enjoys the company of males—I guess he likes to bond. When he isn't asking for food or loving, he's asking to go on the balcony. He would sleep there for days! Topaz is a very loving brother to his family. He teaches strength and Kung Fu to his brothers and sister. Topaz and I have a not-so-typical mother-and-son relationship.

TREBOR LIEBERMAN
ROSLYN HEIGHTS, NEW YORK

Trebie is a lady in every sense of the word. A tabby with a long tail and the whitest of paws, she can be found sunning herself in the garden in summer. Winters find her curled up on a convenient heating duct. She's a junk-food cat who prefers Pounce to real food. Washing her paws in her water bowl is a favorite activity. Trebie loves to watch TV, especially animal programs. If she wants something, she'll poke with her front paw and talk to you until she gets what she's after!

TRIBBLE ZEHR
OMAHA, NEBRASKA

Tribble (formal name: Queen Tribble Precious Bright Eyes I) was born in May 1981. She is a domestic shorthaired tabby cat. She came to live with Scott in January of 1982. She gave birth to a litter of five kittens in March 1982. After weaning her young, she has settled into a quiet life of sleeping, eating, watching the birds, and playing with the dozens of toys she scatters around the apartment from the bean bag she considers a toy pit. She looks forward to the weekly visits from her grandparents, who bring her fresh home-grown catnip.

TRIXIE SRNSKY
THIEF RIVER FALLS, MINNESOTA

Born February 28, 1988, Trixie is your average Himalayan cat. She'd rather groom herself than chase mice or bugs. She only wants to be petted if it's her idea, and she'll jump down when she's had enough. She loves to make mad dashes through the house, sliding on the kitchen floor right into a wall. Trixie's been with me the longest and doesn't take kindly to the new family members.

TUFFY JUSTICE
NORTH ROYALTON, OHIO

Tuffy lives up to his name. He was only four or five weeks old when my son found him, and he hissed and spit when we took him to the vet. He now weighs over twenty pounds and rules our house. He lives with six Siberian huskies and takes nothing from any of them. Whenever people come over, we warn them that he bites. Of course, everyone says, "Cats don't bite," and goes to pet him. They quickly learn we are not kidding. He does not like strangers, but he loves us.

TUFFY ("PUSS") MUSSELMAN
TWELVE MILE, INDIANA

Tuffy is my best friend. She's a fine lady of sixteen years who doesn't know she's a cat. (I'm sure not telling her.) She's a beautiful shorthaired gray-black tabby with eyes like emeralds. Tuffy is always lying on me and prefers I sleep on my side. She loves spaghetti and lasagna. Maybe she was Italian in another life! I've taught her to jump on my shoulder, and she has sure surprised a few people with that trick. She and I love each other with a love that will never end.

TUGGER BEAR
SAN DIEGO, CALIFORNIA

Tugger Bear is a Saudi Arabian cat and is eight years old. Cats in Saudi Arabia are street cats. Tugger was found in the compound of my company. Prayer call was sounded over loudspeakers five times every twenty-four hours. Tugger would respond vocally each time, and although he cannot hear prayer call in the U.S. he still makes the same response two or three times a day. He is very stocky and much stronger than U.S. cats. He is a shorthair with orange and white fur.

VANILLA ("WILLA") LIVINGSTONE
DURHAM, NORTH CAROLINA

Vanilla decided she was ours from the first time she wandered into our yard. Every time we went outside, she would attach herself to us, purring and rubbing against our legs. A cold night arrived and, feeling guilty, we fixed her a box. She knew it was hers without being told and immediately jumped right in, purring nonstop. The next morning she was still there, purring! Two years later she reigns second in command, Ginger being Queen Supreme, and has had three beautiful litters of kittens. Only squirrels, chipmunks, rabbits, and birds fear her. Vanilla, we love you!

VELVET SIZELOVE
ANDERSON, INDIANA

I named my bundle of fur Velvet because she felt like the cloth. This tortoise Persian cat retrieves! I dropped my contact lens and asked her to find it for me. She extended one front paw on the floor and there it was. She understands "no" and will answer when spoken to or called. Just clap your hands and she returns from the outdoors to the inside. She drinks out of a cup and sits like a person on her love seat, placing her paws over the arms. She talks by making reverberations in her throat. She is dearly beloved.

VICKSBURG (A.K.A. BEA, BEABIRD)
MILLINGTON, NEW JERSEY

She was named after the Civil War battle-field. She was a sweet, nutty calico cat, born in the 1960s. She was fond of stealing corn-cobs and chewing them under the kitchen table, and notorious for standing on the stairs and yeow-ing in hopes of attracting a male. Her white feet were often dirty and her whiskers full of cobwebs. She escaped once and was found under the porch. Often she would lie on her back atop her owner's legs. Vicksburg died in the 1970s.

WAFFLES HILL
HOUSTON, TEXAS

Found near a waffle/pancake house on a wet September evening in 1981, Waffles is a pretty, though wimpy tortoise American Shorthair. His classic coloring makes him look symmetrical—on the outside, anyway. A whiner and a pest at times, he can open cupboard doors and sleeps amongst the pots and pans. Occasionally he runs from things only he can see.

WALDO WHISKET ("BISCUIT") HINCK

ST. CHARLES, ILLINOIS

Whisket is a gray Persian cat with gold eyes. Weighing in at about fourteen pounds, he is very distinguished and reminds anyone who forgets! Whisket is the King in his house. He has his dad trained to feed him by hand on command and even has his own feeding mat with his name on it. Whisket enjoys sleeping on his "kitty tree," which he shares with his brothers. He likes the top when he can get there (sometimes he has trouble because he's bottom-heavy). But Whisket's favorite thing in the whole world is his dad, Roy.

WHISKERS
HASKELL, NEW JERSEY

Whiskers, obviously from his name, is an orange tabby cat with an abundance of whiskers. Finicky when it comes to cat food, Whiskers has a definite taste for "people" food. He'll eat anything but chocolate. If given chocolate-chip ice cream, he eats around the chocolate chips; otherwise, the sky's the limit. Occasionally the instigator, he will get our dog Boomer into deep trouble by antagonizing him into a fight and then "blaming" it on him. Although he's Mr. Independent, he shows his sensitive side by hopping up and curling up on his mom's lap for a nice long nap.

WHISKERS GLAVIANO
LAS VEGAS, NEVADA

W hiskers is a white cat with a black tail, black spots, and one black ear. He does tricks for his food. He sits, rolls over, dances, and shakes a paw. When we got him, we lived in an apartment and he wouldn't go outside. We moved to a house and now he's outside most of the time; when he wants in, he knocks on the door. Whiskers likes to play on the reclining chair: he jumps on the back to make it go down, and then he walks to make it go back and forth.

WHISKEY OLSZEWSKI
SYRACUSE, NEW YORK

Whiskey is an oversized galoot with a lovable personality. His kitty disposition is amazingly calm, and he "tolerates" people. He loves to perch on the kitchen table. His best friend is his master, Kenny, but he loves Grandma and Grandpa, too, since they are easily manipulated into extra snacks if his meow is persuasive enough. His favorite activities include eating, sleeping, and window patrol.

WHISPER ("MAUS") VON MERTENS
CULVER CITY, CALIFORNIA

Whisper was born on June 6, 1983. She was the only female in a litter of five kittens. Her fur is white on black, a female version of "Johnny Cat." She is a vocal cat who likes to express her feelings. We consider her our best friend because of her human-like personality. She is affectionate and polite, but can also be jealous and bully our younger male cat, Shadow. Even though she is over ten years old, she is still a kitten at heart and will always be in our hearts.

489

WIDGIE PICKARD
CHATHAM, MASSACHUSETTS

Sixteen-year-old Widgie, a pure gray part-Siamese cat, has a squeak for a meow. He's an outside boy, lounging on porch chairs or chasing rabbits. When inside, he likes to sit on his window perch or be held and rocked like a baby in the rocking chair. While the family is eating, it's common to see a gray paw reaching toward a plate, trying to snitch food from unsuspecting family members. Being affectionate, he prefers sleeping with the family, so he hides under furniture at bedtime to avoid being put in the cellar.

WILHELMINA
MILLINGTON, NEW JERSEY

Commonly called Nookers or Nookie, she was a large calico cat born in the 1970s. She had a pretty, often funny, expressive face. On cold nights, she'd sleep under the blankets. She delighted in climbing into boxes, bags, suitcases, bureaus, and aquariums (empty, of course). She liked to eat cherry tomatoes and chew on apple cores. Her favorite playmate was Bumpers, and the two often slept curled around each other. She died on September 23, 1986 after surgery, and on that day she gave her friend a kind look as if to say, "It's okay."

WILLIE CAT BERANEK
TAMPA, FLORIDA

Willie is a twelve-year-old Maine Coon whose favorite hobbies are eating and sleeping. He's a gentle giant who doesn't know the meaning of the word "aggression." He lives for Christmas and gets positively festive when lying under the tree. After the holidays, he sighs and goes back to sleep until next year. Willie tolerates all creatures who enter his domain, including the feisty Yorkie he's forced to share his home with and whose greatest pleasure is to interrupt his naptime. Willie is truly another name for "love."

WINSTON CHURCHILL NOVIS
BURKE, VIRGINIA

Winston, a.k.a. "Winchen," is the world's most un-independent cat. He does not like to be left alone, and craves constant attention and companionship from his owners. Winston enjoys afternoon walks and sunning himself on the deck. When he wants to go outside, he will bring his leash to his owners. Winston is an excellent bug-catcher, specializing in bees and wasps. At night he insists on sleeping between his owners, or on top of one or the other.

YENTL
SHIPPENSBURG, PENNSYLVANIA

Yentl is an eight-year-old tortie Siamese who looks like melted butter has been dripped on her hand. She is so laid-back that she has acquired such nicknames as "Jello" and "Coma." She is so relaxed that she remains asleep even after falling off the bed. When awake, her favorite "activity" is to be worn around our necks like a scarf. Her means of reaching neck level is to climb like a baby. Yentl's hunting skills consist of keeping the live mouse warm under her belly. Her vocabulary boasts approximately thirty-five words, with a new entry every three to four months.

YODI ("TOAD") KAMPS
POST FALLS, IDAHO

Yodi is a beautiful, black, twenty-four-pound cat. He has green eyes with flecks of turquoise, and they are always wide open. He follows me everywhere. When I sit on the couch, he's right on my lap. He sleeps with me at night and gets under the covers when it's cold. He loves to play out in the yard with his buddy, Maggin, a potbellied pig. He just turned nine years old, but is still a kitten at heart. He is very affectionate, and the perfect pet. Love you, "Toad"!

ZACHARY MATTHEW GAY
DENVER, COLORADO

*Z*achary, a twelve-pound red tabby, loves to play in the bathtub, lie in the sun, and swing from the chandelier when his parents aren't watching. Born on February 29, 1992, "the Zachster" was adopted by his parents, Matt and Lisa Gay, at eight weeks of age. His hobbies include torturing his three feline sisters, watching tropical fish, and chasing flashlight beams around the house (and up the walls). Known for his vainness, he hopes to become a model or actor when he grows up.

ZEKE ("ZEKESEN") PICARD
(A.K.A. POLONIUS, PUSHKIN)
NEW YORK, NEW YORK

I chose Zeke from a xerox of kittens needing adoption because of his big ears. Soon they were only average as the rest of him grew expansively. He's five years old, seventeen pounds, incredibly handsome, charming and creative. When he wants to play, he drops his swan toy at my feet and speaks. His eyes dart from me to the toy: "Get it, Mom?" If I don't, he sighs, takes the swan into the bathtub, and bats it around himself (it ricochets). He's so smart he knows the sound of his food plate hitting the sink: dinnertime. My tender dreamboy.

497

ZEPPELIN THIEL
ANN ARBOR, MICHIGAN

*Z*eppelin is a big, beautiful tortoiseshell cat, with enormous bright green eyes, who loves to wear pearls. For the last fourteen years she has been a companion, best friend, and daughter, all rolled up into one wonderful package. She doesn't care much for most people or animals, but she loves her adopted mother, Julia. In her long life, she has had to endure many different living situations, some hard times, even a trip in the clothes dryer. At this stage in her existence, what she wants most is to be loved and stroked And that's exactly what she gets.